ADHD GO-TO GUIDE

About the Authors

DESIREE SILVA is professor of paediatrics at The University of Western Australia and Joondalup Health Campus. Desiree trained as a doctor in the UK and completed her paediatric specialist training in Western Australia and the Northern Territory. She has a strong interest in neurodevelopmental disorders with over 20 years experience in managing children diagnosed with ADHD, autism, anxiety and developmental disorders. She completed a PhD on the early environmental risk factors and education and justice outcomes for children and youth diagnosed with ADHD. Desiree is a member of the scientific committee for the World ADHD Congress, Neurodevelopmental and Behavioural Paediatric Society of Australasia (NBPSA) and on the professional advisory board for LADS. She is regularly invited to speak at national and international conferences on various aspects of ADHD research. Desiree is the project co-director for the ORIGINS study, a collaborative initiative between the Telethon Kids Institute and Joondalup Health Campus to establish a new birth cohort in Western Australia to provide a better understanding of early pre-programming of neurodevelopmental disorders including ADHD. She is a strong advocate for children and their families requiring support during their journey through life.

MICHELE TONER was the first credentialled ADHD coach in Australia. Starting out as a high school teacher, she has since worked in the corporate, not-for-profit and small business sectors. Her PhD (2009) and Master of Special Education (2001) both focused on ADHD. Currently she works in her private coaching practice, where her clients include executives, adults, parents and students. Michele regularly consults with schools, universities and workplaces to achieve the best outcomes for her clients. She is also a faculty member of the ADD Coach Academy (ADDCA). In addition to her professional work, Michele has been a passionate advocate for people with ADHD since 1995. She has served as Executive Officer, Board President, and Professional Advisory Board member for The Learning and Attentional Disorders Society (LADS WA). She also played a key role in the establishment of the newly formed consumer peak body, ADHD Australia, as a founding Board Member. Michele's solid academic research background and her extensive hands-on advocacy experience allow her to operate comfortably in both the professional and consumer arenas. Currently, she is co-convenor of the Australasian Professionals ADHD Network (AusPAN), and the administrator of several social media support groups for people with ADHD.

ADHD GO-TO GUIDE

FACTS AND STRATEGIES FOR PARENTS AND TEACHERS

DESIREE SILVA AND MICHELE TONER

UWA PUBLISHING

First published in 2017 by
UWA Publishing
Crawley, Western Australia 6009
www.uwap.uwa.edu.au

THE UNIVERSITY OF
WESTERN
AUSTRALIA

National Library of Australia Cataloguing-in-Publication entry:
Silva, Desiree, author.
ADHD go-to guide: facts and strategies for parents and teachers /
Professor Desiree Silva; Dr Michele Toner.
ISBN: 9781742589480 (paperback)
Attention-deficit hyperactivity disorder—Popular works
Attention-deficit hyperactivity disorder—Treatment—Popular works.
Attention-deficit-disordered children—Rehabilitation—Popular works.
Behavior disorders in children—Popular works.
Other Creators/Contributors: Toner, Michele, author.

Cover design by Upside Creative
Typeset in Bembo by Lasertype
Printed by Lightning Source

 uwapublishing

CONTENTS

Chapter 3
Treatment options for ADHD   44

Chapter 4
How can I support my child and family?   68

CONTENTS

Children with ADHD may be talented, resilient and often misunderstood. They can be challenging but are never boring. Parenting requires exceptional skills, which can prove difficult when parents have to manage their own mental health issues, negotiate barriers within the home, school and health system. Understanding and supporting children with ADHD from a young age will improve their education experience, social outcomes in adolescents/adulthood and family functioning.

Desiree Silva, 2017

Before you read a single tip or consider a single strategy in this book, please know this: everything in these pages is written with compassion, and an understanding of how challenging it is to parent a child with ADHD. It requires research, organisation, mediation, advocacy, patience, energy and compassion. Remember to extend that compassion to yourself. You will have days when you feel like 'Superparent', ready to leap the tallest buildings of bureaucracy. And you will have days when you feel like a failure. Celebrate the good days and learn from the others.

Our book is designed for you to flip through and choose an area to work on with your child. Do not feel the need to change everything at once.

Michele Toner, 2017

FOREWORD

Attention deficit hyperactivity disorder (ADHD) is the most common mental health condition in children and is present in most countries around the world. Although there is an abundance of literature on ADHD with plenty of scientific information, this condition remains controversial and often under diagnosed.

Many books have been written for parents about ADHD but most of them are quite scientific, and they can be difficult to navigate, especially if you are a parent with some symptoms of ADHD yourself.

This book is a go-to guide for parents and teachers, providing up-to-date knowledge in a simple, easy-to-read format. It is filled with information your doctor would like to provide but is often unable to do so in the limited appointment time available. This book also gives a framework for how you can manage and advocate for your child in different settings, with or without medication. It summarises evidence to date for medication and alternative therapies, examines commonly held beliefs about ADHD and debunks myths, and gives practical tips to help manage your child with ADHD.

This book has been written by a developmental paediatrician (Desiree Silva) and an ADHD coach (Michele Toner), both of whom are passionate about improving the lives of children with ADHD and their families. They both have over 20 years of experience in the field and recognise the need for this practical guide.

This is a comprehensive and easy-to-read book with up-to-date information for parents, families and teachers of children with ADHD, and also for allied health workers, general practitioners and others who have contact with these wonderful children.

The ADHD go-to guide provides a summary of the science behind ADHD, and the strategies suggested will empower parents and teachers to better understand this common condition. It will help to remove the stigmas associated with ADHD – 'the naughty child', 'poor parenting' or 'the lazy child' – and will provide advice on how to most assist in advocating for your child.

Chapter 1

The basics:
What you need to know about ADHD

Attention deficit hyperactivity disorder (referred to as ADHD or ADD) is a group of symptoms that usually present in childhood and may continue into adulthood, and which primarily affect concentration and attention. A number of children and adults have some level of inattention, distractibility and impulsive and/or hyperactive behaviour, but to meet the diagnostic criteria for ADHD your child has to have a minimum number of symptoms in different settings which significantly impact on their day-to-day functioning. These are summarised in Box 1 on page 7.

Children (and adults) with ADHD often find it hard to sustain attention, especially when doing boring tasks. They rush through tasks just to get them done (or fail to finish them altogether). They can become easily distracted, lose or forget things, interrupt others and/or blurt things out. They will often fidget and find it hard to relax, find it difficult to wait their turn and control their emotions.

They experience these difficulties to a greater extent than their peers, and this may result in them finding it difficult to function at home, in school, socially or in their working environment. If children are distracted, inattentive and hyperactive but are nevertheless functioning well at home and school, they may not be diagnosed with this condition. However, as the workload at school gets more challenging, and/or there is reduced structure and support at home or school, they may meet the criteria for ADHD and benefit from help. Treatment can include advice on home and school strategies, allied support (psychology, speech therapy, occupational therapy and working with an ADHD coach), alternative therapies and social skills, with or without medication.

In general, ADHD is referred to as three subtypes. Your child may have symptoms related to different subtypes at different stages in their life.

- Predominately inattentive: Your child may be described as dreamy and inattentive, with relatively good behaviour, but may be an underachiever. They often have associated learning difficulties.
- Predominantly hyperactive: Your child may be described as hyperactive and impulsive.
- Mixed type: You child displays a mixture of the two types above.

The 'H' in AD(H)D represents hyperactivity, although not all children with ADHD are hyperactive. If your child is described by your doctors as having ADHD, this may mean: ADHD–predominantly inattentive, ADHD–predominately hyperactive, or ADHD–predominately mixed.

ADHD can be a lifelong condition, and 65 per cent of children will continue to have some symptoms as adults. Very often the hyperactivity and impulsivity settles but the inattention may continue as your child grows up.

There are various stages in life where managing ADHD can be particularly challenging, such as puberty, coping with exams, leaving home, making decisions about employment, dealing with relationships and during interpersonal conflict. This guide outlines strategies for helping your child manage their condition through childhood and transitioning into adulthood.

What characteristics may suggest ADHD?

- **Inattention:** Your child is easily distracted, flits from task to task, performs better with one-to-one supervision, loses focus easily, is slow at completing work, and can be difficult to engage and teach. Hence such children do not reach their full potential. Some are distant, dreamy and spaced out and may be described as 'a bee floating from flower to flower but gathering nothing'.
- **Overactivity:** Your child is restless and fidgety, has a need to touch everything and moves from task to task. They may be described as having an 'overwound spring' or being 'driven by a motor'.
- **Impulsivity:** Your child blurts out answers, or does things without thinking.
- **Insatiability:** Your child is rarely satisfied, interrogates people, generates tension and is unaware of when to let a matter drop; 'goes on and on'.
- **Social difficulties:** Your child misreads social cues, can be overpowering and demands attention, 'acting the class clown'.

- **Poor coordination:** Your child is uncoordinated and clumsy, has an awkward flow of movement or has difficulty doing multiple tasks. Their writing is often messy.
- **Disorganisation:** Your child does not recognise 'mess', tends to lose belongings and is often forgetful. Some older children have difficulty structuring their schoolwork, getting started on their homework and organising projects.
- **Variability:** Your child fluctuates between good and bad days, has severe mood swings and can be quite volatile.
- **Difficulty with time management:** Your child has a limited awareness of time passing and may have poor time-management skills.

If the task is highly stimulating, children with ADHD can often focus better and can listen and process information, but their focus may not be consistent over a prolonged period.

Parents sometimes say 'my child doesn't have ADHD as he/she can concentrate when playing his/her computer games for many hours'. This does not exclude children as having ADHD as computer games provide regular reminders or rewards, and are like having a parent or teacher constantly tap them on their shoulder to keep them on task. However, children with ADHD rarely remain attentive through a documentary video or a board game that does not include regular reward and feedback.

You can see from all these symptoms that having ADHD can be challenging for parents, who are often wrongly accused of lacking parenting skills and blamed for their child's so-called 'bad behaviour'. *However, we recognise now that a child's bad behaviour can actually make good parenting appear poor!* It is important to try to understand how your child with ADHD feels, as life can often be challenging and they can encounter many daily negative experiences.

Is ADHD a new diagnosis?

ADHD is not a new condition and has been described in children for over 100 years.

The first description of a disorder that appears to be similar to ADHD in adults was made in 1798 by a Scottish physician, Alexander Crichton. In 1902, ADHD was described in children by the first professor of paediatric medicine in the UK, Dr George Frederic Still. He noted a group of children who were aggressive, defiant, resistant to discipline, who had a poor attention span, poor emotional control and were unable to learn from the consequences of their actions.

In 1937, a psychiatrist called Charles Bradley investigated a group of children with difficult behaviour by taking a spinal tap (lumbar puncture) of fluid for analysis. These children had normal spinal fluid but developed headaches after the procedure, so Dr Bradley gave them Benzedrine (a type of stimulant medication that was used in the 1930s as a nasal inhaler for the common cold). He noticed that their focus and concentration had improved, especially in maths work, so Benzedrine tablets became known as 'arithmetic pills'. In 1944, Leandro Panizzon synthesised methylphenidate (Ritalin), which he named after his wife Rita. It is believed that she found it helped her concentration when she played tennis.

In 1966, the term Minimal Brain Dysfunction was introduced, and referred to children of near-average, average or above-average general intelligence with certain learning or behaviour difficulties ranging from mild to severe. In 1968, 'Hyperkinetic Reaction of Childhood' was described. This relates to children who are severely overactive.

In 1980, the introduction of the *Diagnostic and Statistical Manual of Mental Disorders* was a breakthrough in psychiatry. This book provides information on most mental health conditions and how the diagnosis is made, as there are no specific blood tests or routine scans that can confirm the diagnosis of most of the mental health disorders it describes, including ADHD. There have been several revised editions to the manual, the most-recent being *DSM-5*, published in 2014.

How is ADHD diagnosed?

Like most psychiatric conditions, there is no blood test, brain-wave test or brain-imaging procedure that can reliably diagnose ADHD. ADHD is diagnosed after clinical interview, examination and exclusion of other disorders, assisted by the use of a series of questionnaires. Currently worldwide the diagnosis of ADHD is made using the DSM-5 and/or ICD-10 criteria. A list of these criteria is found in Box 1 on page 7. To meet the diagnostic criteria for ADHD under DSM-5, a child would need to have at least six of the nine symptoms of inattention and/or six of the nine symptoms of hyperactivity/impulsivity present every day or several times a day. These symptoms need to be present in several settings (e.g. at home and at school), and the child must have these symptoms before 12 years of age and for over 6 months, with noticeable impact on their daily functioning. The symptoms also should be out of keeping with their developmental age, which is why it is difficult to diagnose preschool children with ADHD as they are expected to display symptoms of being impulsive, distracted and hyperactive at this age.

Box 1: List of DSM-5/ICD-10 criteria for ADHD

Inattentiveness symptoms your child may display often or very often:

- not paying close attention to details, or making careless mistakes on schoolwork or during other activities
- finding it difficult to keep paying attention during tasks or activities
- not appearing to listen when spoken to directly
- not following through on instructions and failing to finish schoolwork or jobs
- having difficulty organising tasks and activities
- avoiding tasks that require concentrating for long periods of time
- losing things, such as school items, books or shoes
- being easily distracted
- being forgetful in daily activities.

Hyperactivity and impulsivity symptoms your child may display often or very often:

- fidgeting, tapping hands and/or feet, or squirming in their seat
- leaving their seat in situations where staying seated is expected
- feeling restless, running around or climbing in inappropriate situations
- being unable to play or participate in activities quietly
- being on the go, acting as if they are driven by a motor
- talking excessively
- blurting out an answer before a question has been finished
- finding it difficult to wait their turn
- interrupting or intruding on others.

DSM-5 criteria: Your child has had a minimum of six features of inattention and/or six features of hyperactivity over the past 6 months.

ICD-10 criteria: Your child has had a minimum of six features of inattention and four features of hyperactivity/impulsivity over the past 6 months.

Symptoms started before age 12 years.

Symptoms are present in at least two settings, e.g. at home and at school.

Symptoms greatly interfere with school, family or social situations.

At your child's appointment with the paediatrician or psychiatrist you may be asked a detailed history of your pregnancy and the birth of your child, their development and behaviour in preschool, schooling including literacy and numeracy skills, peer relationships, sleep patterns, family history, other medical and surgical conditions, use of alternative therapies and medication, and so on. Your child may undergo a full examination, including a blood pressure measurement, and you and your child's teacher may also be asked to complete a series of questionnaires, which will be used to assist in making a diagnosis of ADHD. Sometimes your doctor may order other tests, such as blood and urine tests (to make sure your child is not anaemic, and has normal iron and thyroid levels), and occasionally chromosome tests and a brain-wave tracing called an EEG may be suggested by your doctor.

Some of the questionnaires used are summarised in Box 2. These ask questions that relate to the core features of ADHD, and other more detailed questionnaires may be used to identify children at risk of other problems that may coexist with ADHD or mimic ADHD. Sometimes these questionnaires are also used to monitor your child's progress.

Box 2: Common questionnaires used by health professionals to assist with the diagnosis of ADHD

Questionnaire	Explanation of questionnaire
ADHD rating scale DSM-5/ICD-10	Consists of eighteen questions specifically addressing only the DSM-5 or ICD-10 criteria for ADHD.
Conners early childhood scale: 2–6 years	Takes 20 minutes to complete and addresses inattention/hyperactivity, emotional regulation, sleep and atypical behaviours.
Conners 3: 6 years and above	This test can measure inattention, hyperactivity, aggressive behaviour, learning difficulty, peer issues and more-specific features relating to the diagnosis of ADHD, oppositional defiant behaviour and conduct disorder. The long version takes 20 minutes to complete and the short version takes 10 minutes.
Child Behaviour Checklist: 4–18 years	120 items that assess behaviour and social abilities.

Continued on next page

Questionnaire	Explanation of questionnaire
Behaviour Assessment System for Children (BASC): three levels of assessment at preschool, primary and high school	Information on behaviour and emotional problems (aggression, conduct problems, anxiety, depression, learning problems), adaptive function (social skills, study skills), externalising and internalising problems.
SKAMP teacher rating scales	10 questions specifically relating to classroom behaviour and attention.
Direct observation	Psychologist observation in the classroom, playground and during association with peers.

Can preschool children be diagnosed with ADHD?

Yes, but with caution. ADHD can be difficult to diagnose in the preschool age group, as young children are still developing their attention skills and are not able to concentrate for as long as older children. If there is a strong family history of ADHD, then there may be an increased suspicion that the preschool child may have it. Diagnosing ADHD in preschool children may lead to other conditions being overlooked (such as global developmental delay, speech delay, autism, hearing loss and vision problems) that would require different management strategies. Management of a hyperactive preschool child can be challenging, although the strategies used are similar whether ADHD is diagnosed or not (summarised in Chapter 4). The Conners early childhood questionnaire for parents and teachers may provide some indication that ADHD may be present, although often with a number of associated conditions such as anxiety, sensory issues, atypical behaviours and sleep issues.

Do children with ADHD have any other mental health issues?

There are a number of other psychiatric conditions, summarised below, that are either associated with ADHD or can mimic ADHD. Having ADHD on its own is very rare, hence it is important to understand what other conditions (sometimes referred to as comorbidities) may be associated with your child's ADHD so they can be managed appropriately.

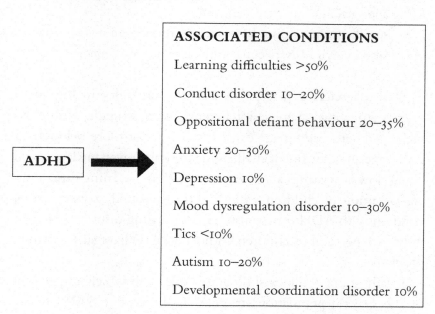

ADHD →

ASSOCIATED CONDITIONS

Learning difficulties >50%

Conduct disorder 10–20%

Oppositional defiant behaviour 20–35%

Anxiety 20–30%

Depression 10%

Mood dysregulation disorder 10–30%

Tics <10%

Autism 10–20%

Developmental coordination disorder 10%

Specific learning disorders

The diagnosis of specific learning disorders requires a child to have persistent difficulties in reading, writing, arithmetic or mathematical reasoning skills during formal years of schooling. Symptoms may include inaccurate or slow and effortful reading, poor written expression that lacks clarity, difficulties remembering number facts, or inaccurate mathematical reasoning. The different types of learning difficulties that are associated with ADHD can occur as a problem in a single area, but more commonly they occur as a combination of the following factors:

- specific learning disorder – with impairment in reading (also known as dyslexia; difficulty reading, writing and spelling)
- specific learning disorder – with impairment in written expression (also known as dysgraphia; difficulty with handwriting and spelling)
- specific learning disorder – with impairment in mathematics (also known as dyscalculia; difficulty with mathematics).

Dyslexia refers to a type of learning difficulty in kids with average to above-average intelligence who struggle with their literacy. Their reading age can be two years or more below their actual age and they find it challenging to write (reversing letters and being slow at writing) and copy information. Learning difficulties are common in children with ADHD – around 50 per cent of children with ADHD may also have a learning disorder, whereas only 5–10 per cent of children without ADHD have such learning problems.

Reading is a complex skill, and is one with which 10 per cent of the general population struggle. To become a skilled reader your child needs to be able to recognise letters and words, have knowledge about rules around letters and sounds, and be able to comprehend what they read. Therefore reading difficulties can present in all sorts of ways – for example, not being attentive, being distracted in class, feeling anxious, having low self-esteem or being embarrassed and angry, to name just a few.

Children with learning disorders can have a high risk of depression as they move into high school. Therefore it is important to identify their problems and provide them with understanding and extra support at home and school.

Oppositional defiant behaviour

Oppositional defiant disorder (ODD) can cause your child to have problems at home and in social, academic or occupational settings. It is characterised by a recurrent pattern of negative, defiant, disobedient and hostile behaviour towards authority figures, which persists for a period of at least 6 months. Approximately 30 per cent of children with ADHD may be diagnosed with ODD.

Not all children who show defiant or oppositional behaviour would be classified as having ODD. Since children pass through many developmental stages as they mature, it is important to understand the differences between a normal child's attempts to defy authority and symptoms of full-blown oppositional defiant disorder.

Children with ODD may display a number of the following characteristics:

- They possess a strong need for control, and will do just about anything to gain power.
- They typically deny responsibility for their misbehaviour and have little insight into how their actions impact others.

- They are socially exploitative and very quick to notice how others respond. They may use these responses to their advantage in family or social environments, or both.
- They can tolerate a great deal of negativity – in fact they seem to thrive on large amounts of conflict and anger from others, and are frequently the winners in escalating battles of negativity.

Conduct disorder

Conduct disorder is seen in 10–20 per cent of children with ADHD. This disorder results in repetitive aggression and antisocial behaviour. Such behaviour tends to be more severe than one would normally expect for that child's age. This condition can also be associated with learning difficulties, so learning and being taught can both be challenging. Having a full assessment and managing other problems associated with their conduct disorder can improve a child's outcomes, especially if the support is provided early. If the conduct disorder and ADHD are not treated appropriately, it can result in significant antisocial behaviour throughout adolescence and young adulthood.

Anxiety

Anxiety is common in children with ADHD and can make their ADHD symptoms worse, although having anxiety may in itself cause difficulties with learning at school and with friendships, resulting in it being confused with other conditions. Anxiety can often present as aggression and heightened mood, including mood dysregulation disorder. There are different types of anxiety disorders, including:

- generalised anxiety disorder
- separation anxiety disorder
- panic attacks and panic disorder
- agoraphobia
- social anxiety disorder (social phobia).

Anxiety disorders can occur in over 20 per cent of children with ADHD. Understanding and supporting your child from an early age with help from specific health professionals (e.g. a psychologist) can greatly assist your child and the rest of the family. The main treatment for anxiety is cognitive behaviour therapy (CBT), although for some children it may be necessary to commence them on anti-anxiety medication which can break the cycle, reduce anxiety and allow your child to function better. If medication is used, it should be in conjunction with positive lifestyle changes and psychological assistance.

Depression
Your child can present with sadness, low mood, negative thoughts and behaviours, difficulty with sleep, irritability, social withdrawal and suicidal thoughts. It is important to be aware that if your child has learning disorders they may have an increased risk of developing depression. It is important that depression is managed appropriately, usually with the support of a clinical psychologist, general practitioner, psychiatrist and paediatrician. Family support is essential. When depression is severe, your doctor may discuss the need for antidepressant medication. Up to 10 per cent of children with ADHD may also have depression, hence it is important that health professionals manage these children appropriately.

Disruptive mood dysregulation disorder

This has recently been recognised as a condition that can occur in up to 30 per cent of children with ADHD and more commonly in boys. Some of the features associated with this condition include severe temper outbursts in response to common stressors, which occur frequently (three or more time per week) and can last from minutes to a few hours; and irritable moods that are inconsistent with the child's developmental age.

Symptoms are usually present for over 12 months and occur in several settings, such as at home, school, with relatives and friends.

This condition can sometimes be confused with bipolar disorder but it is not the same thing. Bipolar disorder can have similar symptoms but they typically last for much longer periods of over 24–48 hours. It is very uncommon for bipolar disorder to be diagnosed in children less than 16 years of age. It is important to recognise mood dysregulation disorder and treat it with behaviour strategies, psychological support, and paediatric and psychiatry input; and for some children, medication can be helpful.

Developmental coordination disorder

Developmental coordination disorder (DCD), sometimes referred to as dyspraxia, describes children who have difficulty coordinating movements (e.g. climbing in the playground, riding a bicycle, catching a ball, getting dressed, and having issues with handwriting, sport and athletic activities).

These children do not have difficulties with movement that can be explained by a general medical condition (e.g. cerebral palsy, stroke or muscular problems). DCD may coexist in over 10 per cent of children with ADHD. It is usually diagnosed with the use of standardised motor testing completed by allied health practitioners after medical assessment.

Features of DCD may include the following:

- Appearing clumsy or awkward in movements compared to their peers (e.g. running awkwardly or holding scissors awkwardly).
- Poor body awareness, such as having trouble determining the distance between themselves and objects and hence bumping into objects or knocking things over, and invading other people's personal space without recognising this.
- Difficulty with or delay in developing gross motor (physical) skills (e.g. running, jumping, hopping, catching balls, climbing, cycling), fine motor skills (e.g. handwriting, doing up buttons, threading beads, tying shoelaces), or both.
- Movement-planning difficulties, such as difficulty planning physical movements into a controlled sequence to complete a task, or difficulty remembering the next movement in a sequence despite being shown or told how.
- Movement-learning difficulties, such as difficulty learning new movement skills and, once learned in one environment (such as in school), difficulty performing the task in another environment (such as at home). Consequently, the child needs to be taught the task again in each new environment.
- Difficulty with activities that require constant changes (e.g. sports such as basketball, netball, tennis).

Autism

Autism describes a spectrum of conditions which can have mild, moderate or severe symptoms. Some of these include poor social skills, especially with peers; difficulty sharing emotions; and not being able to consistently seek and maintain relationships. Children with autism may also have complex sensory behaviours, which can include fussy eating; being fussy with buttons and tags on clothing and with certain types of material; being sensitive to noise and smell; communication difficulties; and repetitive behaviours, preferring a routine and displaying a number of rituals that may change over time. The IQ of children with autism can vary from a superior IQ to a very low IQ. Some children are non-verbal and assessing their IQ can be challenging. As autism is a wide spectrum of disorder, each child can display varying symptom severity, which can change over time. Children with autism commonly have ADHD symptoms, which adds to their challenges at school, at home and with their peers. Children with ADHD may often have autistic-type behaviours, for example, finding it difficult to relate to their peers, but at a level insufficient to make a formal diagnosis of autism. These children benefit from being taught social skills and learning to understand emotions. It is not uncommon for children with autism and ADHD to be trialled on medication in conjunction with home and school strategies, which may help to reduce their symptoms. Some children with autism can be sensitive to medication, hence it may be necessary to try them on different medications, including stimulant, non-stimulant, mood stabilisers, anti-anxiety and antidepressant medications. School support (understanding ADHD and autism, class-aide support, an individual education plan) is crucial to the educational success of children with autism and ADHD.

Tics/Tourette syndrome

Tics are brief, repetitive semi-involuntary movements or sounds that may be related to some problem in the dopamine system of the brain. Tic disorders can be classified as transient tic disorder of childhood, chronic motor tics, chronic vocal tic and Tourette syndrome. In general, tics are either simple or complex. Simple vocal tics may include grunting, sniffing and throat clearing. Simple motor tics may include eye blinking, facial grimacing and shoulder shrugging. Complex motor tics can involve a series of movements such as repetitive touching, squatting or rituals. Complex vocal tics may include repetition of words and phrases, and coprolalia (repeating antisocial words), which occurs in a small number of children with Tourette syndrome. Tics may be present in up to 10 per cent of children with ADHD, where stimulant medication may exacerbate tics rather than cause them. Tics usually decrease in adulthood, although strategies to reduce anxiety may lessen the intensity of tics, especially if they are impacting on the child's ability to function. In some children, medication can be used to reduce anxiety.

Can adults have ADHD?

ADHD has only been recently recognised in adults (although its symptoms were first described in adults over 200 years ago), and it affects around 4 per cent of the population. In the past it was believed that all children would grow out of their ADHD symptoms, so the use of medication usually stopped around 16–18 years of age. This is now known not to be the case, and around 65 per cent of adolescents and adults continue to have some symptoms of ADHD into their mid-30s and beyond. More adults are treated in the USA than elsewhere, and there is some concern that too many people are being treated for ADHD. However, numbers are much lower elsewhere. In Western Australia, for example, only 0.6 per cent of adults are reported as being treated for ADHD.

Symptoms of ADHD in adults are similar to those in children, but as an individual passes through stages in life, environmental demands become increasingly complex. For example, attending university, entering the workforce and becoming a parent all pose new and significant challenges. Adults with ADHD may experience difficulty in focusing, meeting deadlines, following jobs through to completion and sustaining motivation, particularly during tasks which they consider boring or irrelevant. They also describe themselves as being easily distracted; forgetful; disorganised; failing to plan ahead; and performing inconsistently at work, at their studies and on the sports field. They receive more traffic infringements and licence suspensions, particularly for speeding, and are involved in more motor vehicle accidents.

ADHD is most often an inherited condition – adults with ADHD often have children with ADHD. Many parents are diagnosed only after the condition is identified in their child. Research tells us that parenting children with ADHD is stressful. When a parent has ADHD it is even more so. Diagnosis and treatment in parents create better outcomes for children with ADHD.

Psychiatrists, along with other allied health professionals, manage adults with ADHD. Adults can be treated with similar medications used to manage children with ADHD. Medication is not a cure for ADHD but may reduce symptoms, which will help with better functioning. As with children, a multimodal treatment approach is most effective. This can include counselling, psychological assistance and coaching.

Will my child need medication as an adult?

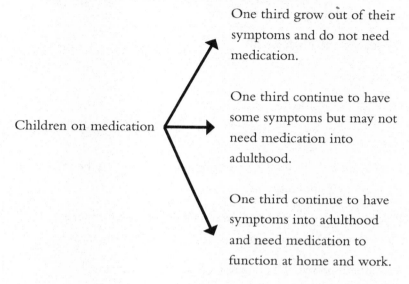

Children on medication

One third grow out of their symptoms and do not need medication.

One third continue to have some symptoms but may not need medication into adulthood.

One third continue to have symptoms into adulthood and need medication to function at home and work.

Planning your visit to your paediatrician or psychiatrist: What information will be useful?

Parents can face a lot of frustration when they try to advocate for their child and negotiate the common barriers to get assistance. The wait time in some areas to see a paediatrician has increased to over several months for assistance with a developmental, behavioural or learning difficulty. Hence it is best to be well prepared so that you and your child get the best information at the time of your appointment. Box 3 gives a list of items you may need for your assessment with your child's paediatrician or psychiatrist, and Box 4 gives a list of other things that would be useful to think about before your appointment.

Box 3: Items you may need for your assessment with your child's paediatrician or psychiatrist

Pregnancy and birth details

School reports

Hearing test results

Vision test results

Parent and teacher ADHD questionnaires (these may be requested prior to your appointment)

Psychology report, which should include an IQ test, literacy and numeracy assessment, classroom and playground observation

Any allied reports: These may include speech therapy, occupational therapy, physiotherapy, social worker, language development centre and child development centre.

Box 4: Useful things to think about before seeing your paediatrician

Family history of ADHD	Diet
Behaviour at home	Getting ready for school in the morning
Behaviour at school	
Behaviour with siblings	Coping with school
Behaviour on family outings	Lunchtime behaviours
	After-school behaviours
How does your child cope with stress and what do they do?	Homework
	After-school activities
How do you parent your child when you are both angry about something?	Who manages to cope with your child best and what do they do differently?
Sleep: bedtime routine, falling asleep, staying asleep, snoring	What does your child do when they are calm?
Electronic use during the day, evening and night	Does your child manage to self-regulate?

Chapter 2

What else should I know about ADHD?

Most children manage very well with their ADHD; however, it is worthwhile sparing a moment to imagine what it must be like to have severe ADHD. You may struggle to fall asleep, and wake up feeling tired and grumpy, only to get told off by your parents and siblings before school, and continue to get corrected or told off by your teachers and your friends and classmates. Your so-called mates at school may bully you, and you finally get home feeling sad and frustrated only to continue to be told off by your family. You feel trapped and seem not to do anything right. Sometimes through all this you might learn to develop some resilience, although it is more likely that you will have an increased risk of anxiety, depression, poor self-esteem and hopelessness, which may continue to impact on your day-to-day life into adolescence and adulthood.

'Children with ADHD need to be understood by their family, teachers and community, who can help raise them to reach their potential.'

Is ADHD different in boys and girls?

In general, boys are diagnosed with ADHD more than girls, at a ratio of 4:1. Boys are more likely to present as hyperactive and misbehaving in class – a well-known symptom of ADHD – hence it is usually identified earlier. Most of the early environmental risk factors (Box 5) are similar for boys and girls; however, boys with ADHD are more likely to have a history of accidents compared to girls with ADHD. Boys with ADHD may also be more likely than girls to have difficulty reading, writing and spelling in primary school.

By adulthood, the ratio of boys to girls with diagnosed ADHD becomes almost equal (1.5:1). This suggests that girls may not be diagnosed in childhood but are more likely to be diagnosed as adults. Girls tend to display inattentive, rather than hyperactive, features of ADHD, hence tend to be quiet and their underachievement may not be recognised during childhood and may be identified only later in life. The boisterous boys (and, less often, girls) who create much class disruption tend to be noticed at a younger age and referred for assessment and treatment. Girls with ADHD may be disadvantaged as they are usually diagnosed quite late, and thus are not provided with appropriate support through school.

Does ADHD exist around the world?

Childhood ADHD exists in most countries at a rate of 3–8 per cent. However, it appears to be on the increase and is being diagnosed more, especially in developed countries. The media have tended to portray ADHD as 'a made-up condition' that is being over diagnosed and over treated, especially in recent years. The reality is that ADHD has been known about for over 200 years, and over the past 20 years there has been a better understanding of this condition, especially when looking at the difference in brain structure and functioning in ADHD and non-ADHD children using special brain scans called functional MRI scans. (These scans are only used in a research setting and not for diagnosing or confirming ADHD.) The diagnosis has increased in areas where children have access to paediatricians and/or psychiatrists who are able to diagnose and treat this condition. Paediatricians, psychiatrists, psychologists, speech therapists, occupational therapists, ADHD coaches, teachers, childcare workers, parents and siblings are better educated about this condition, so the whole community is better equipped to recognise symptoms in children who are struggling at home, school and socially.

Figure 1: Percentage of children diagnosed with ADHD around the world

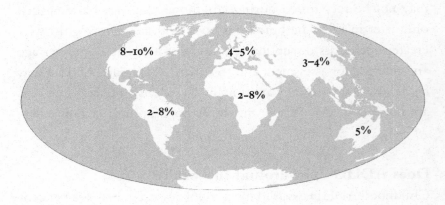

Figure 1 shows ADHD diagnosis rates across the world; however, the number of children affected differs, as different criteria may be used for diagnosis. Acceptance and treatment of ADHD are limited in some developing countries. Instead, corporal punishment (hitting and beating) is used, which does not improve the symptoms of ADHD and may result in long-term mental health problems. Families in many countries around the world do not have access to either non-drug or drug treatments for ADHD.

Is ADHD caused by our genes?

ADHD has a strong genetic inheritance – parents and siblings of children with ADHD are 5–10 times more likely to have been diagnosed with this condition.

Many studies have tried to find a single gene that causes ADHD, but scientists have found many genes associated with it. There is often (in 60–70 per cent of cases) a family history where parents or relatives have ADHD symptoms but may not have been formally diagnosed with this condition.

Researchers have looked at many likely environmental factors and have identified several early risk factors in pregnancy and early childhood that may be *associated with* a diagnosis of ADHD, but this does not mean that any of these factors *cause* ADHD. A list of risk factors associated with ADHD is shown in Box 5.

There is a small increased risk of ADHD associated with being born premature. Smoking in pregnancy may reduce the amount of neurotransmitters in the developing fetus brain, thus increasing the risk twofold of being diagnosed with ADHD. Alcohol is considered toxic to the fetus and drinking large amounts of alcohol in pregnancy has an increased risk of ADHD; studies have shown that lesser alcohol consumption by pregnant mums may also increase this risk. *No alcohol in pregnancy is the safest choice.*

Children diagnosed with ADHD appear to have a much higher risk of having a head injury and these injuries are likely to make the ADHD symptoms worse. Children with recurrent ear infections, tonsillitis and other infections also have a two fold increased risk of being diagnosed with ADHD. It is thought that the infections and other conditions that cause inflammation at certain critical periods of brain development switch on the ADHD gene (this switching on or off of genes is referred to as 'epigenetics'). More work is being done in this area, which may help us understand the genetic and environmental risk factors associated with ADHD.

Box 5: Some environmental risk factors associated* with ADHD

Pregnancy and delivery	Prematurity, smoking in pregnancy, alcohol in pregnancy, pre-eclampsia, infections in pregnancy, prenatal and postnatal depression
Early childhood	Meningitis, encephalitis, head injury, otitis media, tonsillitis, post-traumatic stress disorder

*As noted in the text, 'an association with' does not automatically mean that it *causes* ADHD.

Are children with ADHD different from non-ADHD children?

Children with ADHD have a different brain structure and different amounts of chemicals in their brain compared with children who do not have ADHD.

An ADHD child can have the following:

- A smaller size of certain parts of the brain, although this normally catches up in adulthood.
- A delay in maturation of the outer surface of the brain, especially in the frontal parts, which can make them impulsive and immature. Children with ADHD can have brain immaturity of 2–4 years behind their peers, so you need to take this into account when managing your child at home. Teachers also need to understand this and support children as much as possible.
- A reduction in the neurochemicals dopamine and noradrenaline in the brain. These help the messages to travel through the brain in an orderly fashion.

The images of the brain shown in Figure 2 were developed by an American research team lead by Dr Philip Shaw. The images map out areas of immaturity in the brain of a child with ADHD over time compared with a child without ADHD. There are areas of the brain that have delayed cortical (outer area of the brain) maturation of greater than two years.

Figure 2: Regions of the brain showing delayed cortical maturity in children who are diagnosed with ADHD

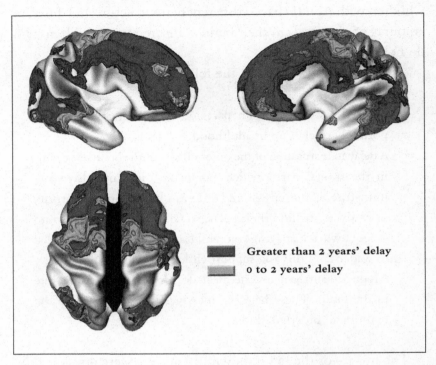

Greater than 2 years' delay

0 to 2 years' delay

How clever can children be with ADHD?

Children with ADHD have a range of IQ scores, from having a superior intelligence to an average or low intelligence. Having ADHD can affect your child's cognitive ability through problems with executive functioning (organisation, planning, memory and processing of information). Your child with ADHD will likely have a number of strengths and weaknesses in their sub-scores, where they may have a high verbal or perceptual IQ score but a low working memory or processing of information. This may result in difficulty calculating a true IQ score, but it gives some indication as to the potential of your child.

The Wechsler Intelligence Scale for Children (WISC-IV) IQ test looks at different measures of cognition, as explained in Table 1.

Table 1: Measures of cognition covered by the WISC-IV test

	Explanation
Verbal IQ	This measures verbal knowledge and understanding obtained through formal and informal education. It also reflects the use of verbal skills to specific situations.
Perceptual IQ	This measures the ability to interpret and organise visual material and to solve problems.
Processing of information	This measures the ability to process information using concentration and hand–eye coordination.
Working memory	This measures immediate memory and the ability to concentrate, especially in numeracy tasks.
Full scale IQ	This can only be calculated if the scores above are similar.

There are a number of parts of the brain that may be affected by ADHD. These include speech and language areas, fine motor areas, coordination, processing of information, short-term memory and time management. Some children and adults may have only a few deficits; others may have a problem in many of these areas. The challenge is to define and understand the areas of strength and weakness so that your child is helped to reach their potential.

What is executive functioning?

The brain can be described as being like an orchestra, where each instrument is a different part of the brain and the conductor is the brain's executive function. The orchestra operates well with a good conductor, but if the conductor is missing, the orchestra would find it challenging to function harmoniously, even though each individual instrument might be played outstandingly well.

Executive function – the conductor of our brain orchestra – is important for everyday activities. It enables a person to take in information, interpret and process the information, and then make decisions based on this information. It will help your child to plan, organise their tasks, prioritise, memorise, manage their time, complete and check their work, and be able to multitask.

Children and adults with ADHD often have an immature or disorganised executive functioning that makes simple tasks more complicated and frustrating.

There are several key skills involved in executive function, but your child may only struggle in some of the following areas.

• **Working memory:** The ability of your child to hold information in their mind and use it to complete a task. They have a hard time remembering directions, taking notes or understanding something you've just explained to them. If your child has trouble with working memory, you frequently may hear 'I forgot what I was going to say.' Children with weak working-memory skills have trouble following multi-step tasks.

- **Self-monitoring:** The ability of your child to keep track of and evaluate their performance on regular tasks. These children have limited self-awareness and understanding of strategies. They often don't know how to check their work.
- **Planning and prioritising:** The ability for your child to come up with the steps needed to reach a goal and to decide their order of importance. These children are easily overwhelmed by multiple tasks. They may have trouble seeing the main idea.
- **Task initiation:** The ability of your child to get started on something. These children often struggle with planning and prioritising tasks, and can be perceived as being lazy. They may be overwhelmed, and do nothing.
- **Organisation:** The ability of your child to keep track of information and their belongings. These children struggle with organisational issues and constantly misplace items. They can't find a way to get organised, even when there are negative consequences to being disorganised.
- **Emotional control:** The ability of your child to manage their feelings by focusing on the end result or goal. Children with ADHD who struggle with emotional control often have trouble accepting negative feedback. They display poor self-regulation and struggle to finish a task when something upsets them.
- **Flexibility:** The ability for your child to roll with the punches and come up with new approaches when a plan fails. Children with ADHD may be inflexible and may interpret suggestions as criticism. They may find it difficult to change course, resulting in frustration and panic.

Can my child grow out of their ADHD?

Yes, but the majority will have some ongoing symptoms into adulthood. It is generally accepted that about one third of children with ADHD will have significantly fewer symptoms and function well in adulthood; one third may have reduced symptoms and can manage without treatment, although they still may need some psychological support; and one third will need to continue taking medication and will need ongoing support. In the past, doctors felt that by 18 years of age, children would have outgrown ADHD and would not require further treatment. This is now known to be incorrect, and there is a better understanding of the 2–4-year delay in brain maturation. During school years there is a clear structure to the day, but when children with ADHD leave school this structure is lost, as it is expected that, like their non-ADHD peers, they will be mature enough to organise their life. This does eventually happen for the majority, but not without good support and understanding, which is sometimes necessary into their thirties and beyond when the core symptoms of ADHD are found to reduce significantly.

How may my child with ADHD grow up?

In a very supportive family and community environment, children with ADHD can blossom and reach their potential. However, we do recognise that some children with ADHD, even if they are very bright, can struggle through school. There is a high risk of school failure, rejection by their peers, poor social skills, low self-esteem, antisocial personality and increased risk of smoking and substance-use disorders, especially if they are not supported and treated appropriately. They can also have sleep and mood difficulties, and although they can be fussy with their eating, obesity is common in adulthood. Children and families also report high levels of stress; however, some research studies have shown that children and adolescents who are treated with medication are less likely to use recreational drugs, smoke or enter the justice system. They do better at school and have a better quality of life in general.

Do children with ADHD have sleep issues?

Yes, parents commonly report sleep problems in their child with ADHD, and poor sleep patterns can continue into adolescence and adulthood.

There are a number of different types of sleep problems associated with ADHD, which are listed below. Understanding which type may be affecting your child will help management of their sleep problems. Medication may either improve or worsen your child's sleep; however, sleep problems are often present before starting stimulant medication. There are a number of conditions that may disrupt your child's sleep irrespective of ADHD; although having ADHD may make this problem worse.

- **Behavioural sleep problems:** Electronic equipment use prior to sleep, bedtime resistance, excessive noise, excessive light, temperature changes (being too hot or cold), uncomfortable bed, insomnia, anxiety and sleep associations.
- **Medical conditions that may impact on your child's sleep:** Sleep obstructive apnoea, ADHD, anxiety, epilepsy, asthma, allergies, overweight, prescribed/unprescribed drugs, restless leg syndrome (which may be associated with low iron level).

Although behavioural approaches have been effective in managing sleep problems in children with ADHD, some children may benefit from using long-acting synthetic melatonin. Melatonin is important for sleep regulation and is made naturally by melatonin receptors in the eyes and other parts of the body. Problems with sleep onset may be related to insufficient melatonin production or anxiety. Excessive light may also suppress melatonin production, which is often found when electronic equipment is used before bedtime. Synthetic melatonin (slow release) appears to be very effective in managing children with sleep initiation difficulty. In Australia it is only available on prescription, but in Europe and the USA it can be bought over the counter. Melatonin can also be compounded into a liquid form, which is easier to administer. Talk to your doctor and pharmacist about this.

What should you tell your doctor about your child's sleep problem?

Think about the questions listed in Box 6 before seeing your doctor, as they may be able to provide a better understanding of the underlying issues which may contribute to your child's sleep difficulties.

Box 6: Questions that your doctor may need to ask about your child's sleep

- What time does the child usually go to bed at night and wake in the morning?
- What is the child's usual bedtime routine?
- Does the child have the same bedtime routine on weekends?
- Does the child wake at night?
- Does the child worry a lot about things?
- What are the usual working hours of the parents?
- Does the child share a bedroom with siblings or parents?
- Are there computers/TV/games consoles in the child's bedroom?
- How does the parent manage sleep difficulties?
- Does the child drink caffeinated drinks or eat chocolate after school?
- How do the parents and child want to manage their sleep problem?
- Does your child snore and wake up several times at night?
- Is your child very restless at night?
- Is your child on medication?

Is electronic addiction a problem?

Computers, games consoles and gaming, the internet and social media are part of everyday life for children and adolescents. While computer use is problem-free for many children, the activation of the reward centre of the brain during an activity like gaming makes it highly pleasurable, and can lead to addiction in susceptible children. Computer-game addiction in children with ADHD is being increasingly recognised. Excess computer gaming has been shown to increase depression, anxiety and social phobias, and to affect your child's sleep cycle and school performance.

The proposed criteria for internet gaming addiction is summarised in Box 7, where clinically significant impairment or distress is indicated by the presence of at least five of the listed symptoms in a 12-month period.

Box 7: Proposed criteria for diagnosing internet gaming addiction

Symptom	Description
Preoccupation with internet games	Thinking about previous game activity; anticipation of the next game
Withdrawal symptoms when gaming is taken away	Typically irritability, anxiety, sadness, but with no physical signs of pharmacological withdrawal
Tolerance	Need for increasing amounts of time engaged in internet games
Loss of control	Unsuccessful attempts to control the participation in internet games
Loss of interest	Previous hobbies and entertainment are neglected, except for internet gaming

Symptom	Description
Continued excessive use of internet games	Happens despite knowledge of psychosocial problems
Deceit about the amount of internet gaming	Has deceived their family members, therapist or others
Use of internet games to escape or relieve a negative mood	May be feeling helpless, guilty or anxious
Relationship or career jeopardised	Has jeopardised or lost significant relationships, job or educational/ career opportunity due to internet gaming

It is important to consider reducing time spent on computer games for children with ADHD in order to avoid excessive gaming and computer gaming addiction in the future.

Are there other conditions that can mimic ADHD?

Yes, there are some children who have difficulty at school, appear easily distracted and have difficulty completing tasks, yet may not have ADHD. There are a number of conditions that may mimic ADHD, and your doctor will consider them when assessing your child. Some of these conditions are listed in Box 8; however, it is important to note that a number of these problems can coexist with ADHD.

Box 8: Conditions that may mimic ADHD

- Sleep problems
- Problems with vision, hearing and/or auditory processing
- Epilepsy
- Acute or chronic medical conditions (e.g. chronic lethargy, hypothyroidism)
- Poor nutrition
- Excess or chronic alcohol consumption
- Illicit drug use
- Depression, anxiety, conduct disorder, oppositional defiant behaviours (although these are often present with ADHD)

It is believed that some of these conditions can exacerbate ADHD symptoms. What needs to be determined is whether any of the conditions are the primary cause of the child's problem or are a result of having ADHD. A careful history, and specifically addressing some of these issues, may reduce the symptoms of ADHD.

Sleep problems

Being chronically sleep deprived can result in poor concentration at school and restless, irritable daytime behaviour. See page 35 for more information about the effects of sleep problems in children with ADHD.

There are a number of conditions that can affect your child's sleep. Some of these include night terrors, obstructive sleep apnoea, asthma, allergies, excessive light, excessive noise, an uncomfortable bed, being too cold or too hot, bedtime electronics use and lack of a sleep routine. Having ADHD can also affect a child's ability to fall asleep, even when the child is not medicated. Obstructive sleep apnoea usually presents with loud snoring and intermittent stopping of breathing during sleep. The best way to diagnose this condition is by performing a sleep study. A referral to an Ear, Nose and Throat (ENT) specialist may be required, and they may suggest the child has their tonsils and adenoids removed. This may improve sleep, as well as daytime behaviour and concentration.

Epilepsy

Epilepsy can present in different ways at various ages, and can sometimes mimic ADHD. Absence seizures are a form of epilepsy that occurs around primary school age. The teacher may notice the child having a brief blank spell or appearing as if they are in their own world. The child does not lose consciousness but has no memory of that brief event. This may be mistaken for ADHD, but with a good history and an EEG (an electronic measure of brain activity) this condition can be diagnosed and effectively treated.

Problems with hearing, auditory processing and vision

Children who have impaired eyesight or hearing can miss instructions in the class and at home, have trouble reading, and become disengaged and disinterested. They may also disrupt the class and develop behaviour problems. Children with glue ear or chronic ear disease may have impaired hearing in one or both ears, which can make learning very difficult. A number of these children also develop auditory processing difficulty, where they can hear but have difficulty processing information and find it difficult to follow simple instructions, especially when there is background noise. Auditory processing difficulty does improve with age, but there are a number of strategies that the schoolteacher can use to help these children learn more effectively. Auditory processing is best tested between 7 and 11 years of age.

It is important that children who are being investigated for ADHD and learning issues have their hearing and vision tested.

Poor nutrition

Having the correct foods to fuel brain development is very important, especially in children. It is recommended to eat a wide variety of foods that are naturally colourful and varied in texture and flavour. Protein foods, such as eggs, cheese, tofu, red meat, white meat, poultry, game, fish and seafood, milks and yoghurts, nuts, dried beans and lentils are needed for the metabolism of neurotransmitters and hormones, and for repair, growth and development. Carbohydrate foods, such as bread products, rice, legumes, lentils, grains (such as couscous, oats, polenta, quinoa, bulgar, barley and buckwheat), pasta and noodles, alternative milks, dairy foods, fruits and juices, and some vegetables are needed to fuel the brain and muscles in children and adolescents.

Children who don't eat an adequate amount of food may fail to thrive due to inadequate caloric intake. Inadequate dietary intake may result in macro- and micro-nutrient deficiencies. For example, anaemia can result in lethargy, poor concentration and various behaviours. Children who have iron deficiency are also at risk of cognitive or learning developmental delays, poor concentration at school, daytime sleepiness and night-time restless leg syndrome.

Drugs and alcohol

There are a number of prescription drugs used to treat various conditions (e.g. ADHD, epilepsy) that can cause inattention and distraction. Stimulant medications used to treat ADHD may affect sleep, which in turn reduces daytime concentration and increases irritability. Some of the medications used to treat epilepsy can also cause symptoms similar to ADHD, such as reduced concentration, irritability and poor focus. Some antidepressants and medications used to treat anxiety may have a sedative effect and cause sleepiness, which may mimic symptoms of ADHD.

Some antihistamines used to manage allergies may also increase daytime drowsiness. Illegal drugs like cannabis can lead to a reduced attention span and difficulty focusing.

Alcohol can also cause symptoms similar to ADHD. Drugs and alcohol may also worsen symptoms in children with ADHD. Random urine drug testing is recommended for children on medication for ADHD over 16 years of age, although sometimes this testing can be performed if there is a history of unusual changes in personality, friendship changes or known substance misuse. When urine drug testing is performed, drugs consumed up to 3–4 weeks earlier may be detected.

Chapter 3

Treatment options for ADHD

There are a number of drug and non-drug treatments that should be considered when managing a child who has ADHD and is not functioning in the home and school environment. Although medication is not the only treatment for ADHD, it is often very effective in reducing the core symptoms of ADHD (inattention, distraction and/or hyperactivity), and may improve self-esteem, school performance, family functioning, interaction with friends, memory, performance, mood and sleep. A number of non-drug treatments, which may assist your child, are described below. Chapters 4–7 also provide a number of strategies that may benefit your child, family and school to best manage your child's ADHD.

Managing ADHD can be a complex journey where good communication with your doctor and other allied professionals will help with finding the perfect balance for your child.

Non-drug treatments

Treatments other than medication should be considered for all children and adolescents diagnosed with ADHD. This section provides a summary of the evidence to date of what might be helpful.

Behaviour

There are a number of behaviour interventions that appear to be very successful, especially those reported by the parents rather than the teachers. These include positive parenting, social learning, cognitive behaviour therapy, life-management coaching skills, improving family relationships, parent training and school-based behaviour programs. Combining behaviour strategies and medication has proved to be very successful. Although behaviour methods reduce core symptoms of ADHD by only a small amount, they have a number of other useful benefits such as improving parenting, improving family and peer relationships, helping with daily functioning and organisation skills, and helping children who have an associated conduct problem.

Diet

Unhealthy dietary patterns (usually high in saturated fat, refined sugars, and processed food and low in fruit and vegetables) are often associated with ADHD. There is compelling evidence that what we eat has an effect not only on our weight but also on our mood, behaviour and immune system. Research has focused on our gut bacteria which are directly affected by what we eat. Recent studies have shown a reduction in ADHD symptoms for children who consumed a Mediterranean diet which is primarily plant based foods such as green vegetables, fruits, legumes, nuts and whole grain.

Certain types of dietary fats can also affect our focus and concentration, these are divided into saturated, monounsaturated and polyunsaturated groups based on their chemical structure. One subset of polyunsaturated fats is called essential fatty acids (EFAs) – 'essential' because they must be part of the diet as they cannot be made in the body. EFAs have several important functions for our cells, brain and immune system. They can be divided into two groups: omega 3 and omega 6. The omega 6 group is found throughout the body, whereas the omega 3 group is concentrated in the brain cells. Some studies have found a higher level of behaviour problems, temper tantrums and sleep problems associated with omega-3 deficiency and higher rates of respiratory tract infections and antibiotic use associated with omega-6 deficiency. Having a good, healthy diet, which includes fresh fish, is the best way of getting EFAs. EFAs have been shown to provide some benefit in concentration for children with ADHD, although they are less effective than stimulant medication. Some children with ADHD are fussy eaters and have various sensory issues, so may be unwilling to take fish oils. Since the evidence for their efficacy is low, children with ADHD should not be forced to take supplementary fish oils, although it is important to look at ways of getting fresh fish and foods containing EFAs into their diet.

Reducing artificial food colourings can have a reasonable effect on improving ADHD symptoms, especially if a child is known to have food intolerances. This is more apparent when parent information about a link between colourings and symptoms is used rather than teacher information. In general, artificial food colourings are not considered healthy and may affect other aspects of growth and development.

A specific elimination diet called the Feingold diet eliminates artificial colouring, flavouring, preservatives and naturally occurring salicylates, and was once recommended for children with ADHD. However, the research evidence does not fully support the claims made for this diet, and there may have been flaws in the design of the original study which may have affected the findings on the effectiveness of this diet.

In general, diet is important and may affect some aspect of behaviour and brain development. Healthy eating from a young age, and good nutrition in pregnancy, should be encouraged.

Neurofeedback

The brain emits different types of waves, depending on whether your child is asleep, in a dream state or daydreaming and in a focused state. Neurofeedback helps your child to improve focus and reduce distraction by teaching your child to change their brain waves into a focused state using a computer screen, which provides visual feedback on how they are focusing and which parts of the brain are being activated. Studies on neurofeedback have shown a small improvement in core ADHD symptoms, and larger effects on the working memory, which can be associated with ADHD. More work is required to determine which type of ADHD may respond better to neurofeedback treatment.

Allied support

Types of allied support include speech therapists, occupational therapists, physiotherapists and psychologists. Each may have individual benefits for your child, depending on their symptoms and age.

- **Speech therapists:** can assist children who are struggling through school with their communication, language, reading and social skills.
- **Occupational therapists:** can assist younger children who have sensory issues, including anxiety, via a sensory diet, which is not a food diet but a series of specific exercises and changes in their sensory environment. Some children may benefit from improving hand strength, handwriting and core strength using strategies provided by an occupational therapist.
- **Clinical or school psychologists:** can provide invaluable support to assist with behavioural problems, anxiety and depression associated with ADHD; this includes cognitive behaviour therapy for children with oppositional defiant behaviour and conduct disorder.
- **Dietitians:** Accredited Practising Dietitians are trained to assess, advise and manage all nutrition and dietary concerns. It is important to have supervision if doing elimination test diet trials for food intolerances, which can coexist with ADHD, to prevent nutritional inadequacies.
- **Physiotherapists:** children with ADHD who have developmental coordination disorder may benefit from physiotherapy for balance, coordination and core strength.

ADHD coaches

ADHD coaches work with children and parents to set goals, identify their strengths, increase their knowledge of ADHD, develop self-awareness and improve social skills. The coach and client work together to design and implement practical, effective strategies that enable them to manage everyday challenges, which often include time management, organisation and procrastination. Regular sessions provide accountability and support as new skills are learned and new routines are put in place.

A word of warning: coaching is not a regulated industry, which means that anybody can call themselves a coach, regardless of their level of training, or lack thereof. Choose your ADHD coach wisely. They should be a credentialed member of the International Coach Federation (ICF) and the Professional Association of ADHD Coaches (PAAC), or actively working towards those credentials under a credentialed mentor coach.

Tutoring

Tutoring is an important part of managing children with ADHD – especially those that have specific learning difficulties. Specialised reading programs can teach phonological awareness, and when started early may be key to reducing anxiety, and depression, which may be exacerbated in children with ADHD who struggle through school. Children with ADHD tend to miss information, especially if they are distracted in a classroom, so their learning can be improved with smaller class sizes or individual tutoring.

Outdoor activities and exercise

Outdoor activities can be structured or unstructured play. Unstructured play has been shown to improve confidence and reduce stress and anxiety in children, although this not specific to ADHD. Regular contact with nature has been shown to reduce ADHD symptoms. Regular exercise, especially outdoors, can improve concentration and reduce fidgetiness. Studies have shown that it may increase blood flow to the brain and enhance brain connectivity, which may improve concentration.

What medications are available for my child?

> *Studies have shown that there is often a delay of 2–4 years from diagnosing ADHD to commencing medication, as parents prefer to try all possible alternative approaches before using medication. The media tend to portray quite the opposite, where they suggest that parents insist on medicating their children, which is seldom the case. Medicating your child does not mean you have failed as a parent.*
>
> *It is encouraging that effective medication is available, along with home and school support, to manage your child with ADHD.*

Stimulant and non-stimulant medications are the most effective ways of treating the core symptoms of ADHD. Although these medications have been well studied and their positive effect noted in large research trials, there is still plenty of misinformation, scepticism and concern regarding treating children with medication for ADHD.

If your child has diabetes, thyroid problems or asthma, there would be no doubt that evidence-based treatments should be used.

Why shouldn't the same apply to children with ADHD, when their condition can cause significant problems in daily functioning (including a higher rate of accidents and injury), education and self-esteem? One can argue that not treating moderate to severe ADHD is irresponsible. Education at every level, from individual and family to school, community and government, is necessary to ensure that medication treatment is used in conjunction with other non-pharmacological treatments to provide the best opportunity for children with ADHD.

Stimulant medications

Stimulants such as methylphenidate and dexamphetamine are the most widely prescribed medications for ADHD and are very well tolerated. The number of children treated using stimulant medication has increased twentyfold over the last 20 years. The treatment of ADHD is very well monitored; for example, in Western Australia only paediatricians and psychiatrists can make the diagnosis of ADHD, and need to notify the Health Department which holds a register of all children and adults diagnosed with this condition. Every script of stimulant medication dispensed is also registered – monitoring of medication use is very strict.

Stimulant medications are usually first prescribed to determine if the drug is effective. If the medication helps your child's focus but the effects do not last or there are side effects, the medication should be changed. If medication needs to be given several times a day, it can be difficult for the child, parent and school, so a longer lasting stimulant medication is suggested. Table 2 describes the properties of stimulant and non-stimulant medications available in Australia, including their peak effect and duration of action.

Table 2: Common medications used to treat ADHD

Medication	Frequency	Peak Effect	Duration of Action	Administration
Dexamphetamine Sulphate (Dexamphetamine)	1–2 times per day	1–3 hours	5 hours	Small tablet; crush or swallow whole
Lis-dexamphetamine (Vyvanse)	Once daily	1–3 hours	12 hours	Dissolve in water or swallow whole
Methylphenidate Short Acting (Ritalin)	2–3 times per day	1–3 hours	2–4 hours	Small tablet; crush or swallow whole
Methylphenidate Long Acting (Ritalin-LA)	Once daily	3 hours	6–8 hours	Sprinkle contents of capsule on food or swallow whole
Methylphenidate Extended Release (Concerta)	Once daily	3–4 hours	8–10 hours	Capsule; swallow whole
Atomoxetine (Strattera)	Once daily	5 hours	24 hours	Capsule: swallow whole

The two main types of stimulant medication prescribed in Australia are methylphenidate (Ritalin short- or long-acting) and medicinal amphetamine (dexamphetamine or lis-dexamphetamine). The main action of stimulant medication is at the neurotransmitter level, making sure that dopamine, and to a lesser extent noradrenaline, levels are elevated within the brain cells. These improve the ability to send messages across the brain connections and lead to better organisation. The choice of which medication is used in the short and long term is dependent on a number of factors which your doctor will discuss with you.

The Australian government mandates that for methylphenidate products, the short-acting medication has to be tried first, and if it does not have significant side effects and the child requires a longer period of cover, it may be changed to the intermediate-acting or longer-acting medications.

Parents are often confused by dexamphetamine (medical amphetamine) and methamphetamine (ice). Although there are small similarities in part of the molecule, they are very different drugs. Dexamphetamine is used to treat ADHD and narcolepsy; methamphetamine is addictive, toxic and should be avoided.

Non-stimulant medication

Atomoxetine is the non-stimulant medication available in Australia. This medication was first developed as an antidepressant, and although studies found minimal antidepressant effect it was found to improve concentration. This medication mostly acts on the noradrenaline pathways and to a lesser extent on the dopamine pathways. It may take 6 weeks to 3 months to notice its full potential. This medication is given only once a day, and improves symptoms over a 24-hour period.

Atomoxetine does not have the immediate effect that stimulant medications have, but it may have benefits for children who are very anxious, have tics (which may be exacerbated by stimulant medication) and develop side effects on stimulant medication; and for adolescents and adults who take recreational drugs.

Figure 3: Scale of effectiveness for different treatments to reduce the core symptoms of ADHD

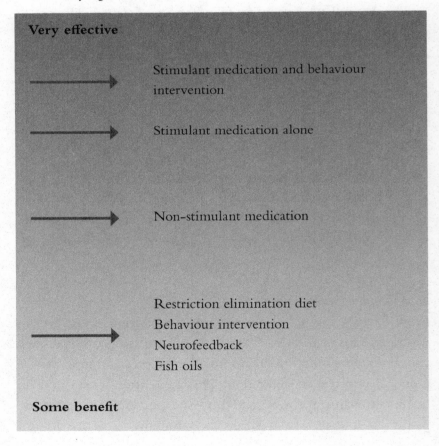

Other medications

The medications listed in the table below can be used in conjunction with stimulant and non-stimulant medication or on their own. They can help with hyperactivity, anxiety, mood stability and sleep disruption.

Table 3: Other medications used to treat ADHD symptoms

Medication	Description
SSRIs (selective serotonin reuptake inhibitors)	These are often prescribed for anxiety and/or depression in children with ADHD. They act on a chemical in the brain called serotonin. The SSRIs include drugs such as fluoxetine (Prozac/Lovan) and sertraline (Zoloft). Their side effects may include increase in weight, but more importantly they may occasionally cause activation, agitation or increase in self-harm thoughts (suicidal ideation) in a small group.
Risperidone	This is an antipsychotic agent used to treat schizophrenia and manic depression in adults. It is also used to stabilise mood in children diagnosed with autism. Risperidone may also be used in children with very labile moods; however, it needs to be used with caution, especially in overweight children, as it can significantly increase their appetite.

Medication	Description
Clonidine	This is an anti-anxiety, calming medication, which was initially used to reduce blood pressure. It may help to calm children before sleep or reduce hyperactive behaviour. Blood pressure monitoring is important when using this medication. If given as an accidental overdose (both parents separately give the tablet as their child's night medication), it may cause severe problems with blood pressure.

What are the side effects of medication?

Although there are potentially a number of side effects from medication, some of these problems may already be present in children with ADHD before they start medication. About 50 per cent of children who are started on medication do not have any problems tolerating medication. Thirty per cent of children may have mild side effects or an exacerbation of features that already exist. The majority of them will eventually settle, but 20 per cent of these children may need to try several medications before a suitable one is found. It must be noted that 20 per cent of children do not respond to stimulant medications, and other non-pharmacological treatments need to be used along with advocating for your child.

A list of side effects for stimulant and non-stimulant medication is shown in Box 9. Non-stimulants have less effect on appetite and sleep disruption. The major side effect of non-stimulant medication, which occurs rarely, is suicidal ideation. This is a side effect that can occur when taking antidepressant medications, and atomoxetine has some antidepressant properties. It can happen in the first few months of taking medication, so you need to be aware of this possibility and stop medication if it occurs. You need to be aware that some children with ADHD have symptoms of anxiety and depression (see Chapter 1), and these symptoms, along with suicidal ideation, may be present before medication is started. If this is the case, your doctor will closely monitor your child and may also suggest psychology input.

In rare instances, Atomoxetine can cause reversible liver damage (1 in a million), which presents as jaundice (yellow discolouration to skin). If this occurs, the medication should be stopped immediately and medical attention sought.

Box 9: Some side effects of stimulant medication

• Insomnia or trouble sleeping	• nightmares
	• Increase in anxiety
• Talks less with others	• Irritability
• Decreased appetite	• Headaches
• Stomach-aches	• Sad/unhappy
• Drowsiness	• Prone to crying, usually when medication is wearing off
• Increased blood pressure	• Aggressiveness/hostility, especially when medication is wearing off
• Increased heart rate	
• Dizziness	
• Palpitations	• Exacerbation of motor and vocal tics

Some of the issues listed in Box 9 may be present before medication is started, and may get better or worse on medication. It is important that your doctor monitors this closely and you discuss other options if necessary. Stopping stimulant medication suddenly is not a problem, but it is really important to discuss all side effects with your doctor.

Questions commonly asked about medication

Is stimulant medication overprescribed?

This is a common concern and is often discussed in the media. What we do know is that ADHD is present in approximately 6 per cent of children in Australia, whereas only 1.25 per cent of children in Western Australia are prescribed stimulant medication. We can conclude from this that not all children need stimulant medication to manage their ADHD, and that stimulant medication is not overprescribed in Western Australia. In the USA, up to 20 per cent of boys have been reported to have ADHD symptoms and over half are prescribed stimulant medication. Studies are currently underway to further explain the discrepancy in level of medication prescription between the USA and other countries.

Is stimulant medication safe for my child?

Ritalin first came on the market in 1944, so its side effects are well studied. The most common side effect is appetite loss, followed by sleep disruption and mood disruption, including increased activity when the medication wears off. The longer lasting medications appear to have fewer side effects, but this may not always be the case. The problems associated with medication are usually mild and short term. To date, no serious long-term effects of stimulant medication have been found, apart from the rare changes in heart rhythm which may occur in children who have an underlying heart problem. There are some processes in place to report and monitor drug side effects where any adverse drug reaction is reported to the pharmaceutical board and investigated.

Does my child have to take medication every day?

Regular medication is the best choice for treatment, but there are a number of children who find that they only need medication to concentrate at school, so they tend not to take medication over the school holidays and sometimes over the weekend. If the medication helps with their behaviour and social functioning, it is probably best for them to remain on regular medication.

What should I do if my child refuses to take medication?

It is not uncommon for teenagers to make their own decisions about medication, among other aspects of their life. It is best to find out why they don't want to take it, as some older children are able to better articulate that the medication makes them feel sad, low, quiet, not sociable or over-serious. This may allow for a discussion about trying a different medication. Sometimes it's best for the teenager to understand how their body reacts to medication so they can develop some insight into the benefits.

How can my child swallow medication?

Swallowing medication can be very stressful for children who may be sensitive to the taste, or feel the tablet or capsule may get stuck in their throat, and also for parents who are keen to ensure their child takes the medication prescribed by their doctor. Table 2 on page 52 contains a list of medications available in Australia and the form in which they are available.

In summary:

- Ritalin (short-acting) and dexamphetamine are small tablets, which may be crushed and given on a spoon with water, yoghurt, jam or any food that your child likes.
- Ritalin LA (long-acting) comes in capsules that can be opened and the beads sprinkled on any food.
- Lis-dexamphetamine comes in capsules that can be opened and the contents dissolved in water, juice or yoghurt.
- Concerta comes in small capsules that need to be swallowed whole and must not be crushed or cut.

Tips for helping your child swallow a tablet or capsule

- Take a sip of water, then place capsule or tablet on middle of tongue and take another gulp of water.
- Place the capsule or tablet on some yoghurt, jam or slimy food and wash it down with a gulp of water.
- Remember that you must not be stressed when teaching your child to swallow. Provide plenty of praise and discuss with your doctor other alternative medications that are more 'swallow friendly'.

How can medication be started?

There are several ways your doctor may begin medication. One common suggestion is to start on short-acting Ritalin, taking half a tablet in the morning and half at lunchtime. This can be increased to get the best concentration during the daytime, when your child is usually at school. The medication lasts for 2–4 hours depending on the individual child. Some children can become more distracted, anxious, teary or aggressive as the medication wears off. A longer-acting medication may then be tried. This will provide cover for most of the day with less of a rebound effect as the medication wears off. You may not get such a dramatic immediate effect when using the slow-release medication compared with the short-acting medication. Your doctor may consider starting your child on dexamphetamine or lis-dexamphetamine, which are intermediate and long-acting medications. With all medications to treat ADHD the general rule is to 'start low and go slow'.

How can symptoms be controlled?

In order to get the best treatment tailored to your child's needs, they may need to trial 2–4 different types of stimulant and non-stimulant medication. Each child will metabolise the medication differently and may show a different pattern of response or side effects. This may be distressing for parents but it is best to find out which medication best suits your child. The difficult times to manage are mornings, after-school homework and the evenings before bed. Some children may require both a short- and long-acting medication to get better control. Some children only need medication to cover their concentration at school, and don't take medications over the weekend and/or school holidays. These children often have the predominately inattentive type of

ADHD. Children who have the mixed type or predominately hyperactive type may require medication over the weekend and school holidays. There is no necessity for 'drug holidays', unless your child experiences mild side effects so may be better off not on medication outside school hours.

Treatment of ADHD may target different areas of the brain to help your child function better. The research may show that medication specifically improves working memory, which may help your child scholastically, especially with their numeracy skills. Behaviour management does not necessarily improve working memory or processing of information, but it nevertheless remains crucial in helping your child function better in the home, among their peers and in society.

How do these medications work?

> The working of a brain can be described as a car battery with millions of cells all filled up with distilled water (neurochemicals). If there is insufficient distilled water in some of the cells the car will not work properly, and similarly in the brain the messages can be confused or lost.

Each brain cell needs neurotransmitters like dopamine and noradrenaline to transfer messages across the brain in a smooth manner. Once the neurotransmitters are released into the synaptic space, they are captured back into the cells and reused. Children with ADHD have a reduction in neurotransmitters (dopamine and noradrenaline) within their brain cells. The medications all target this area but work slightly differently. Methylphenidate (Ritalin) inhibits the reuptake of these neurotransmitters from the synaptic space back into the presynaptic neurone, hence increasing the

brain message

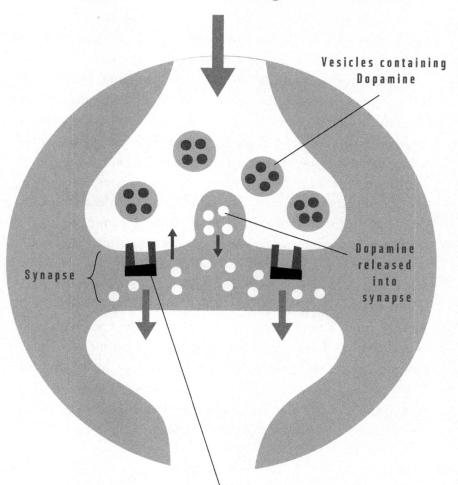

Vesicles containing
Dopamine

Dopamine
released
into
synapse

Synapse

RITALIN and Dexamphetamine block
the reuptake of dopamine
hence increasing dopamine in the synapse

concentration of neurotransmitters in the synaptic space. This results in an increase in dopamine, and to a lesser extent noradrenaline, in the brain synaptic space. Dexamphetamine works in a similar way but also stimulates the release of dopamine and noradrenaline out of the presynaptic neuron into the synaptic space.

Lis-dexamphetamine is an inactive pro-drug where the dexamphetamine is attached to an inactive protein called lysine. Once the drug is absorbed into the bloodstream, the lysine protein detaches from the lis-dexamphetamine. This medication may reduce the abuse potential of stimulant medication.

Atomoxetine is known as a non-stimulant and does not usually have a stimulant effect or have the same side effects as a stimulant. Unlike stimulant medications, which affect the dopamine pathways, Atomoxetine predominately affects the noradrenaline pathways.

Atomoxetine is a selective noradrenaline reuptake inhibitor, which means that there is more noradrenaline neurotransmitter in the brain cells. This benefits your child by improving their concentration. Atomoxetine is usually started at a low dose and slowly increased over 2–3 weeks to the recommended dose; however, it can still take up to 3 months to see its full benefit. Atomoxetine also can be effective over a 24-hour period and is usually given once a day in the morning, but if it causes tiredness this medication can also be given at night.

What may be noticed when medication is commenced?

The following positive comments from parents or their child with ADHD have been reported by paediatricians:

- 'Within 2 days of starting medication the teacher was gobsmacked! From not being able to write he became the best in his class.'
- 'Even the dog likes him.'
- 'He was invited to a party for the first time.'
- 'He has so much more confidence.'
- 'He is smiling and happy.'
- 'I feel my brain has unblocked; it is not muddled anymore.'
- 'I always thought I was stupid but I now believe I am clever.'
- 'She can now start and complete her work and then have time to play with her friends.'
- 'She has stopped bed wetting.'
- 'We can now go on a family outing.'
- 'There has been no more damage to our home.'
- 'The school is delighted and will not let him come to school unmedicated.'
- 'She was asked to her first party.'
- 'Thanks, my life has changed.'
- 'My husband and I separated two years ago as the stress of living with my son was too much for us. We are now back together and our family life seems much calmer.'
- 'He is now starting to learn at school. Prior to this I felt the school was babysitting him and providing damage control.'
- 'I can now remember things in my brain.'
- 'He doesn't chew on his T-shirt anymore and makes better eye contact. We are so pleased that he has become part of our family.'

The following negative comments from parents have been reported by paediatricians:

- 'He lost his appetite completely.'
- 'She was a good sleeper but now is not going to sleep till after 11 pm.'
- 'He is more anxious.'
- 'She looks like a zombie.'
- 'The teachers and my family think he looks depressed.'
- 'He looks sad and tends to be more sensitive in the afternoons.'
- 'She is able to concentrate well at school but her behaviour is still a nightmare at home.'
- 'He seems sad since starting the medication.'
- 'She is much quieter and not interacting with friends as much.'

Stimulant and non-stimulant medications are more effective than non-drug treatments (behaviour intervention, cognitive behaviour therapy, neurofeedback, restricted elimination diet and fish oils) in reducing the core symptoms of ADHD (Figure 3). However, behaviour intervention and cognitive behaviour therapy can help with family and peer interactions.

Box 10: Pills don't teach skills

Management of ADHD needs to have these basic strategies in place, with or without medication:

Improve your and your family's knowledge of ADHD

Have a peer support group

Have an individual education plan at school

Understand and manage other conditions associated with ADHD

Try cognitive behaviour therapy

Try family therapy

Support children to develop organisational and planning skills

Try ADHD coaching support

Seek allied support where necessary

Seek support from your GP, paediatrician and/or psychiatrist

Help your child develop good food choices and regular exercise

Increase time spent outdoors

Ensure good sleep habits

Manage your child's screen time

Chapter 4

How can I support my child and family?

Mary's story

My daughter Claire has the inattentive type of ADHD, so she's a daydreamer. She also has anxiety. At school she was always pleasant and compliant, and nobody suspected that she was struggling on several fronts. We moved her to a new school in year 6, chosen for its smaller size and student-centred learning. On her first day, as I was introducing myself to some of the mothers, I was warned to keep my daughter away from a boy in her class called Tom, because 'He's got ADHD'. Of course, the first thing I did was rush off to find Tom's mum. That was the start of a friendship that has lasted 20 years.

Andrea and I supported each other. I was there for her when the primary schoolteacher complained about Tom's behaviour for the hundredth time. She was there for me years later when the high school science teacher accused me of being the cause of my daughter's anxiety. We educated ourselves and each other and swapped notes each time a new routine worked – or didn't. When members of our extended families failed to support our children we became each other's families. Together we looked out for our kids, taking it in turns to attend camps and excursions. So, Andrea was there to calm my daughter's anxiety, and I was there to redirect her hyperactive son. We have shared our burdens over countless cups of coffee, and the odd glass of wine.

Our children have supported each other too. As Claire once said: 'Tom helped me to chill when I got too sensitive today; and I persuaded him to throw away the cigarette lighter he brought to school'.

What are the everyday effects of ADHD?

The executive-function impairments in the brain that are associated with ADHD show up in every aspect of your child's life. It is important to recognise them as serious difficulties that will persist across the lifespan for many, although they may seem trivial to most. An understanding of what is (or is not) happening in your child's brain will help you to choose from the strategies provided in this book and to target them for the best results.

- **The inability to pause.** Challenges associated with ADHD are often not due to a lack of skill or knowledge. Instead, they are caused by an inability to demonstrate skills or to draw on knowledge as and when required (at the point of performance). For example, your child may know exactly how to get dressed for school, but some distraction could derail the process. Your child is unable to stop, make the decision to ignore the distraction, and return to the task at hand. Whatever captures their attention will become their priority. Strategies and reminders must always be targeted at the point of performance.

- **Time blindness.** The ADHD brain does not have an internal clock. In order to understand time, your child needs to see it. They will lose sight of time passing when busy with enjoyable tasks, and time will appear to drag on endlessly when tasks are challenging. They are able to work towards deadlines that are close in time, but lose sight of deadlines that are further out. As a result, many projects are completed at the last minute. Hindsight and foresight are also impaired in children with ADHD. This results in 'mistakes' being repeated despite consequences.

- **Memory blanks.** While the long-term memories of many children are excellent, they often struggle to hold information in their short-term or working memory. For example, mental arithmetic can be challenging, even for those who excel at mathematics, and verbal instructions are ineffective. Once again, it is essential to externalise memory requirements, preferably at the point of performance. Visual prompts are necessary to remind your child of what needs to be done at the time and place required.

- **The inability to self-motivate.** ADHD brings with it a deficit of motivation. It is dependent on the immediate environment, with immediate consequences and rewards being the most effective incentives. Video games, for example, provide immediate rewards and consequences. Homework, on the other hand, provides no immediate reward, and has possible consequences sometime in the future. It is important to devise systems for getting tasks done that include immediate rewards, and to teach your child to use fun activities as a reward for completing challenging tasks.

- **Emotional flooding.** Difficulty controlling emotions is a strong characteristic of ADHD, and this affects thoughts and actions. Your child will struggle with self-soothing, resulting in angry outbursts, brooding or mental meltdowns.

- **The inability to plan and problem-solve.** This will cause your child to stall when faced with challenging tasks. Assignments and projects, for example, seem impossible to complete when the first step is not clear. Chunking and creating a hands-on plan that is visually presented are important.

Find out how ADHD affects your child

- While children with ADHD have many common characteristics, each child will be affected differently by their symptoms. In addition, conditions that co-occur with your child's ADHD will create a unique set of challenges.
- Take the time to learn about all conditions impacting your child, and observe their effects. This will enable you to design appropriate accommodations for your child at home, and also to advocate on behalf of your child in a meaningful and focused way.
- Take time also to document those strategies and environments that work for your child. This will enable you to pass that information on to teachers, friends and family.

What support do I need?

Parenting is challenging. When a child has ADHD the task of parenting becomes even more so, and a specialised set of skills is required. It is vital for parents to take care of themselves as they take care of their children. Having a child with ADHD puts a strain on parents' relationships, so take care of your relationship as well.

- **Practise self-care.** Parenting a child with ADHD is demanding, time-consuming and expensive. As parents, we always put the needs of our children first. However, parents need to take care of themselves if they are to take care of their children.
- **Find your tribe.** Parents dealing with ADHD are sometimes judged harshly by our society, which often does not have a clear understanding of the challenges facing ADHD children and their carers. Fortunately, there is wonderful support to be found from other parents in similar situations. Find those parents and spend time with them.
- **Take care of your own mental health.** There are higher levels of anxiety and depression in parents of children with ADHD. Seek professional help and take care of your mental health if this is becoming an issue for you.
- **Work together.** Conflict between parents is common. A consistent approach from both parents makes the ADHD parenting job easier for all. Take time to ensure you are on the 'same page', and are backing each other at all times. If necessary, get professional help to coordinate your approaches and resolve conflicts.

Who do I tell and what do I say?

Some people will be extremely supportive when they hear that your child has ADHD; others may not. This may apply to friends, to members of the community, and also to extended family members.

- **Choose who to tell.** There are people who need to be told about your child's diagnosis of ADHD, such as teachers and some family members. Aside from those who need to know, be discerning about disclosure. Most people think they know about ADHD due to media coverage which is often inaccurate. Therefore, telling them that your child has ADHD may cause them to make assumptions based on their understanding or misunderstanding of the diagnosis.

- **Name the symptoms, not the condition.** For those who may not be supportive, avoid naming ADHD. Instead, talk about the symptoms and how best to handle them. For example:
  - 'Dennis can be very active at times. We handle that by giving him something physical to do.'
  - 'Sharon is a daydreamer sometimes. We get her attention by tapping her on the shoulder.'
  - 'Michael can be overly emotional at times. We handle that by distracting him – giving him something else to focus on.'

- **Offer to share information.** ADHD is extremely well researched. Share links to research-based websites and factual articles or books with those who need to know. Inform them that much of the internet-based information on ADHD is sensational and based on uninformed opinions.

- **Establish boundaries.** As a parent of a child with ADHD you may find yourself on the receiving end of well-meaning advice or criticism. Put firm boundaries in place with those whose advice or comments are unhelpful and unwelcome. Let them know that you have consulted experts on matters of diagnosis and treatment. If appropriate, let them know what they can do to support you and your family.

How can I talk to my child about ADHD?

Your child is more than an ADHD diagnosis. He or she is an individual with unique qualities. Be curious with your child, and discover together what those qualities are. Then, help your child to recognise how ADHD affects the way they operate. There is no 'one size fits all'. ADHD coach Barbara Luther recommends that you record information about your child in a document all about them. This will become their DIY (do it yourself) manual for managing their ADHD in the future.

Suggestions for the DIY manual

- **About me:** my strengths, my interests, my learning styles (how I understand information, how I remember what I learn at school, how I learn at karate, swimming, soccer or ballet)
- **Focusing tips:** how I get focused, how I stay focused
- **Homework routines:** routines that work for me, and how to reward myself
- **Assignment tips:** tips to get me started, and to help me finish on time
- **Social tips:** what to remember when I'm with friends, activities that I do well with friends
- **Ideas pages:** things I can do when I'm bored, activities I can choose instead of computer games
- **Stress:** how I can recognise when I feel stressed, and how I can manage this (e.g. using mindfulness).

How can I promote my child's self-esteem and resilience?

Children with ADHD face many challenges. Their shortcomings and 'failures' are constantly pointed out, and they are told regularly that they could 'do better if they tried harder'. Acutely aware of their challenges, they are often unaware of their strengths and talents.

In conjunction with the self-discovery discussed above, work with your child to create a positive framework within which they can operate and flourish.

Build a strong relationship with your child

- As the parent of a child with ADHD, you may feel driven to teach your child as much as you possibly can in order to provide them with the skills they will require to navigate life. While it is important to do that, it is also important to build a relationship with your child.
- Spend some time each week just hanging out together and make a rule for yourself not to provide any teaching or corrections during that time. Know that your child will be learning from you just by spending special time with you.

Wellbeing

Extensive research by Martin Seligman, the founder of the Positive Psychology movement, has identified the following categories for developing wellbeing in children and adults, which, in turn, increases self-esteem and resilience: **P**ositive emotions, **E**ngagement, **R**elationships, **M**eaning and **A**ccomplishment (PERMA).

- **Positive emotions.** More complex than that yellow smiley face, positive emotions include joy, gratitude, serenity, interest, hope, pride, amusement, inspiration, awe and love. Introducing these emotions into your child's life on a regular basis will increase their positivity and optimism.

  Exercise: Choose a positive emotion and find ways for your child to experience it on a regular basis. For example, point out amusing aspects of situations, and encourage your child to do the same; list three things you are grateful for each night for two weeks; draw their attention to an awe-inspiring sunset.

- **Engagement.** We are engaged when we are absorbed in an activity, relationship or project. An important part of engagement is identifying and using signature strengths.

  Exercise: Help your child to identify an activity that absorbs them, and encourage them to pursue it on a regular basis.

  Discover your child's signature strengths with the free VIA survey at http://www.viacharacter.org/www/#nav.

  Point them out to your child each time you see them in action.

- **Relationships.** Meaningful social interactions are important for everybody. Children with ADHD, however, often struggle to have relationships with their peers.

  Exercise: Every child needs a mentor. Foster a meaningful relationship between your child and a relative or friend. Work on your own relationship with your child, and model behaviours they will need to learn in order to form other relationships.

- **Meaning.** We are at our best when we dedicate our time to something greater than ourselves.

  Exercise: Encourage your child to be involved in a cause, such as wildlife conservation, regeneration of bushland or fundraising. Attend community activities with your child.

- **Accomplishment.** Everybody is good at something. Children with ADHD sometimes feel as if there is nothing they do well. It is important to set achievable goals and celebrate their achievements in order for them to experience this sense of accomplishment. It is also important to point out what they are doing well, as they may discount it.

  Exercise: Start a success diary for your child. Make a note each day of even the smallest successes they have achieved. For example: '*I remembered to take my library books to school. I handed my science assignment in on time.*'

Resilience

Resilience is the ability of individuals to 'bounce back' from bad experiences. Developing your child's self-knowledge, self-esteem, positivity and overall wellbeing will increase their resilience. Other opportunities to promote your child's ability to bounce back include the following:

- **Practise problem-solving together when challenging situations occur.** If your child is struggling with an issue, take time to investigate all of the possible options for resolving it. You can model this skill when you face challenges in your own life.

- **Empower them to fight their own battles.** Self-advocacy is an important skill for your child to develop. Again, model the skill as your child's advocate and support them as they learn to stand up for their rights.

- **Model and encourage optimistic thinking.** Pessimistic thinking can be changed. Take time to point out to your child when they are being pessimistic and make them aware of potential positive outcomes to their problems.
- **Allow your child to make mistakes and to learn from them.** Parents are hardwired to protect their children. This protection needs to be balanced, combining the encouragement of some risk-taking and protection from harm. Turn mistakes into opportunities for learning, asking your child what they will do differently next time and supporting them to implement their new wisdom.

Expect and accept inconsistency

'The only consistent thing about ADHD is inconsistency.'
— *Russell Ramsay*

A frustrating aspect of ADHD for children, teachers and parents is inconsistency, even when children are medicated. It is difficult to understand that they may be capable of a task one day, but not the next.

- **Accept that inconsistency is part of ADHD.** Your child is not being lazy if they have forgotten a skill previously mastered.
- **Celebrate the successes and add them to the success diary.** Use them to inspire your child towards future successes. Never ask your child: 'Why couldn't you do this yesterday?'

- **Help your child to accept inconsistency.** If you are frustrated by this aspect of ADHD, consider that it may be even more frustrating for your child. Instead of asking: 'Well you did it yesterday, what happened today?', try reminding them that they have succeeded at the task before and will do so again.

Hone your organisational skills

- **Children with ADHD need organised parents.** Some parents are easily able to be organised; others find it challenging. If you are not an organised parent, get support from a friend or ADHD coach in order to improve your skills. It is important to plan routines and activities ahead of time to minimise stress and conflict, and to maximise results.
- **Is there a parent with ADHD?** A child with ADHD has a 50 per cent chance of having a parent with ADHD. Many adults are diagnosed with ADHD as a result of their child's diagnosis, recognising similar traits in themselves. If you suspect that you or your partner may have ADHD take the necessary steps to have it identified and managed, for your sake and that of your family. (See 'Can adults have ADHD?' on page 19.)

How can I create and follow ADHD-friendly family routines?

Parents in ADHD families often describe their lives as chaotic. Simple routines can help to conquer this chaos, and also teach your child essential skills. The two most important routines to nail down first are morning routines (getting ready for school) and evening routines (getting ready for bed). In order to establish a routine you need five things: a list, a timer, an instant reward, consistent practice and patience.

Making the morning routine easier

- **Sit down with your child and compile a list** of everything that needs to be done in the morning, and then encourage your child to convert that list into a format that suits them. For example, if they are artistic, or respond to visual prompts, have them draw or find pictures to represent what they need to do. If they respond to verbal instructions, have them record their list as a voice memo. It is best to do the list in the same order each morning, in order to create a routine.

- **Decide with your child how much time they need to complete the list**, and ensure that they plan their waking-up time accordingly. Use a timer to keep them focused on their list. Suggestions include the humble wind-up kitchen timer, visual timer apps, apps that include a list and timer, or a playlist of songs tailored to fit into the agreed time.

- **Agree on an instant reward** that your child will get when they have completed the assigned list in the assigned time. This is not a bribe, but an incentive at the point of performance. Remember to be specific about the reward. Choose a reward that will not be costly, and one that will motivate your child. For example, a football card for their collection, a texta for their art kit, some time to play with Lego or My Little Pony toys, or a pebble or coupon that can be swapped later for computer time. Be warned that the reward will lose its appeal at some stage, and will need to be replaced. Most rewards can be recycled, so keep a list of what works in your child's DIY manual.

- **Provide scaffolding** for your child each morning by getting them out of bed and starting their timer. Monitor their progress, and when you see them off task send them back to their list and timer.
- **Be patient**, and remember that one of the hallmarks of ADHD is inconsistency. This means that your child may nail the list one day, and then struggle the next. Resist the temptation to get negative on bad days, and remember to celebrate the good days.

Making the evening routine easier

- **Make a list with your child of things to be done before bedtime.** Include chores such as cleaning up after dinner if that is expected. Also include preparation for the next morning in the form of putting the correct school clothes out.
- **Manage screens, including TVs, and use them as a reward for list completion.** For example, if your child spends some time on the computer, or watching TV, before going to bed, ensure that everything on the list is done first, including showering and chores.

Tips that may improve your child's sleep

- Set clear bedtime and wake times and be consistent.
- Avoid caffeine (drinks, chocolate bars) after 3 pm.
- Make the bedroom a digital-free zone. Take all digital equipment out of their room (no TV, iPad, mobile phones; charge computers for school in a central living area).
- Ensure the bedroom is cool, quiet and relatively dark.

- Keep the bedtime routine calm, with no stimulating activities during the hour before bed.
- Avoid letting your child nap during the day.
- Ensure your child spends time outside during the day with sun exposure and exercise, as this can help to regulate the sleep clock.
- Teach your child relaxation and try mindfulness exercises before bedtime.
- Eat healthily and reduce preservatives, sugar and fat.
- Get regular exercise, which can improve sleep.
- Shift the body clock: set the target sleep time, then check what time your child actually falls asleep; bring this time forward every night by 15 minutes until the target time is reached.
- Try compounded melatonin to help your child to fall asleep and to regulate their sleep cycle. Talk to your doctor for further information.

How can I manage my hyperactive preschool child?

Although this can be challenging for parents and family, hyperactivity in the preschool age group can be considered as normal behaviour. Some of the strategies outlined below are a helpful start to managing your child's symptoms, irrespective of whether they have ADHD.

- Try positive parenting, which includes providing verbal praise and attention immediately for good behaviour and ignoring bad behaviour where possible.
- Set consistent limits and age-appropriate expectations for your child.

- Give your child clear and consistent instructions, making sure they have heard and understood them.
- Maintain structure and routine at home.
- Establlish a good diet and good sleep habits.
- Help your child understand that their actions have consequences.
- Reduce electronics use as a 'baby sitter'.
- Anticipate negative behaviour and distract your child to prevent it occurring.
- Make time to play with your child and allow your child to lead the play, including having unstructured play.
- Reduce sensory stimuli (e.g. noise, loud music or bright colours).
- Don't lock horns with your child, as they very quickly learn from your actions.
- Talk to your child about their behaviour when you are both calm. You could start the conversation with 'I love you very much but it made me sad to see you so upset...'
- Discuss with your doctor the need for a developmental assessment, allied support such as speech therapy, psychology and/or occupational therapy, which can include a sensory diet (Chapter 3). Some children may also benefit from medication.

How can I manage transitions?

Because of executive-function impairments, children with ADHD have great difficulty switching their attention from one task to another. For example, making the transition from outside play at recess to working at a desk in the classroom can be a longer process for them than for their peers. It is also particularly challenging when they are required to switch their attention from a highly stimulating task to one that is less engaging. As an example, asking a child to switch off a computer game and get ready for bed has created meltdowns in many families. In addition to the daily transitions children are required to make, there are also major transitions, such as moving to a different year of school, moving from primary to high school or high school to university or TAFE, and moving house.

- **Prepare your child for transitions by issuing warnings.** Have an agreement with your child that you will issue warnings to indicate the end of an activity. If they are engaged in a fun activity, for example, give them a 10-minute warning that the activity will end. Provide a visual timer to enable the tracking of the warning period. When the time is up, insist on the activity ending, as per the agreement.
- **Facilitate transition to a new activity with bridging routines.** For example, sleep hygiene practices provide a bridge to bedtime, and focusing routines provide a bridge to homework or a new period at school.
- **Prepare your child for major transitions with rehearsal and reconnaissance.** For example, if your child is moving to a new school, visit the school with them before the new term begins in order to familiarise them with the layout of the school. Request a copy of their timetable in advance to help them identify their classrooms. Rehearse new bus routes together before they take the bus alone.

What about siblings?

Children with ADHD take up much of a family's time and resources. It is important, however, to bear in mind that their siblings have special needs of their own. Issues for non-ADHD siblings include the following:

- Feeling overlooked or unfairly treated. Parents devote most of their time to their sibling, who appears to 'get away' with bad behaviour.
- Being embarrassed by their sibling's behaviour at school and at home, sometimes causing them to avoid inviting friends to the house.
- Feeling worried about their sibling, or responsible for them.
- Feeling that they are being attacked, verbally or physically, at times by their sibling.

Strategies for dealing with these issues include the following:

- **Family meetings.** Encourage family conversations where each child is heard and respected. Teach children to air their grievances and express their feelings in a respectful manner, without name-calling or blaming. Ensure that all children are heard, and teach assertiveness skills where necessary. Small but regular communication goals can be set for all family members.
- **Encourage cooperative activities**, such as board and card games and Lego building. Use them as an opportunity to acknowledge and reward cooperation.
- **Recognise each child's uniqueness.** Avoid having your child with ADHD labelled as the family's 'problem'. Discuss the challenges associated with ADHD, and also highlight

their strengths. Take time to acknowledge the strengths and challenges of the non-ADHD sibling, who may be dealing with issues of their own.

- **Talk about fairness vs. preferential treatment.** Parenting skills need to be adjusted for children with ADHD. For example, sometimes allowances need to be made for ADHD-related behaviours, and some are best ignored. If non-ADHD siblings understand the reasons behind this approach, they are better able to view it as fair. By the same token, non-ADHD siblings deserve fair treatment and should not be expected to tolerate inappropriate behaviours from the sibling with ADHD. Choose your battles.

- **Give each child their own space**, where they can have timeout from siblings, and teach all siblings to respect that space and timeout when requested. Extend this to 'play dates' if necessary.

- **Give each child some individual time with you.** Organise an activity away from the rest of the family where you can devote your attention to them alone.

- **Seek professional help if necessary.** Psychologists who specialise in ADHD-related family issues should be considered if issues remain unaddressed, or if they escalate.

Chapter 5

What can I teach my child?

Anne's story

As parents, the backpack we carry when our journey starts with our child can place a heavy burden on the shoulders. My backpack grew heavier over some years at each parent–teacher meeting, with Hugh described as 'not concentrating on his work, forgetful, going off task, and not listening'. I was doing everything I could think of to help him. Then a wonderful young teacher reached in and lifted a brick from my backpack: 'Anne, do you think Hugh might have Inattentive ADHD?' The relief was immense for me.

After extensive testing, a paediatrician prescribed medication. The backpack got lighter but the emotional backlash from family and friends was at times brutal. As Hugh's ability to focus on schoolwork increased, his results improved. But organisation, time management and social interactions remained problematic. So we tried coaching, where he worked on strategies that help him manage his personal routines, plan his own study paths and cultivate friendships. The load was lightened once again.

At our last parent–teacher night, we moved from teacher to teacher to be told our son was in the top 10 per cent of each subject. A first! What a wonderful academic achievement and great result for all his hard work, but it didn't seem to compare to the comments describing what a great person he was: 'Willing to try everything, someone you can trust, always putting forward a great effort even when he might not be so good at something, and if he is good at something, helping others who might be struggling. This is a wonderful young man'.

The backpack was empty that night!

I would love to say, 'Pop a pill and go to a coach and this magic cloak will appear and all will be perfect', but it isn't true. It also needs a team, made up of family and friends, and a supportive school environment. You will still need to push, then run ahead and pull – but you will get them over the lifeline.

How can I teach my child to pause?

There is no pause button in an ADHD brain. Whatever captures your child's attention will become their priority. We've discussed the importance of reminders at the point of performance. In addition, by teaching your child a simple mindfulness activity, you can demonstrate the power of the pause. With practice, it will become easier, so find a way to rehearse often. For example, strategically placed stickers around the house could remind them to practise pausing. The Three Sighs exercise by meditation teacher Eric Harrison is ideal:

1. Take a deep breath, opening the chest. Sigh as you let the breath go without pausing. And wait until you need to breathe in again.
2. Take a second big in-breath, combined with a yawn. Breathe out with a sigh, and wait.
3. Take a third breath, sigh and pause for as long as it feels natural.
4. Breathe normally and notice how you feel.

This short and simple exercise can be modified once your child has mastered it. Even a single mindful sigh can be effective. In the school environment, breaths can be released through the nose instead of sighing, so that it's not quite so noisy. A sticker on the school diary or locker could prompt a pause at school.

How can I teach my child to manage time?

Someone once said, 'Time is the thing that keeps everything from happening all at once. Time parcels moments out into separate bits so that we can do one thing at a time.' In ADHD, this does not happen. In ADHD, time collapses. Time becomes a black hole. To the person with ADHD it feels as if everything is happening all at once. This creates a sense of inner turmoil or even panic.

The individual loses perspective and the ability to prioritize. He or she is always on the go, trying to keep the world from caving in.

— Dr Ed Hallowell

ADHD causes 'time blindness', and this creates challenges on several fronts:

- **Time flies when they're having fun.** This concept is experienced in the extreme when a child has ADHD. Activities that are enjoyable and stimulating tend to absorb their attention for hours on end, but children experience the period as being very short.
- **Time drags when tasks are boring or challenging.** Your child will be genuinely surprised to hear that they have spent a mere 15 minutes on homework, when it felt more like an hour to them.
- **Tasks are harder to complete when there is no visible cut-off time.** Starting homework, for example, without a visible timeframe makes it more onerous, as it appears to have no end.
- **Anticipating the passing of time is difficult without a visual aid.** Telling your child that they need to be ready to leave the house in 15 minutes is irrelevant without some physical representation of that period. Sending your child to timeout for a specific time without a visual representation of time passing can create anxiety as the period may seem endless.
- **Anticipating a date in the future is a challenge.** This can, for example, cause problems with homework delivery. Typically, distant deadlines slip off the radar until they become urgent, and many homework assignments are completed the day before they are due.
- **Time required to complete tasks is underestimated.** This causes children with ADHD to overcommit, or start too late to meet a deadline.

In order to make time manageable it needs to be made visible – and sometimes audible as well. Here are some strategies to help you make time visible for your child:

- **Visual timers** can be downloaded onto smartphones or tablets. They typically represent a period of time as a circle, and the colour of the circle changes as time passes. Showing your child what 15 minutes looks like as they are preparing to leave the house makes it easier for them to use that time well. Visual timers are also useful for dividing larger tasks into short bursts, or 'sprints'.

- **Countdown or wind-up timers** are an effective alternative for parents who wish to avoid screen-based timers. Traditional wind-up timers make a ticking noise as they count down the minutes, and some children use that sound as a reminder that time is passing. For those bothered by the ticking, battery-operated countdown timers can be positioned next to your child who can monitor the minutes counting down.

- **Calendars** make time visible in the long term. The humble wall calendar is a great tool, enabling your child to see due dates at a glance. Used effectively, the calendar creates an instant picture of where your child is in time, and how that relates to the timing of important dates. Crossing off each day as it passes or having a clear marker draws their eye straight to the current day. Failing that, your child could spend some time in front of the calendar wondering where they are before becoming distracted and wandering off, none the wiser.

- **Electronic calendars** are an effective alternative, particularly for older children who use computers at school. However, they must remember to view an entire month at a glance when using this option. While calendars on smartphones are great for recording information and setting reminders, they are too small to provide that monthly overview, and should be synced to a computer calendar for that purpose.

- **Weekly planners** can be used very effectively in conjunction with a monthly calendar. Seeing a detailed week at a glance enables your child to allot their time. Using colour coding for different 'zones' of their life, they start by entering existing time commitments, such as extracurricular activities, family functions and social plans. This provides a clear picture of the time available to them for homework and assignments, and they are less likely to leave homework until the night before. Weekly planners can also provide a visual reminder of items required at school each day – sports bag, library bag, etc.

How can I teach my child to be punctual?

Tardiness is common in people of all ages with ADHD. By teaching your child to be punctual for school and other commitments you will be doing them a great service. Adults with ADHD who do not learn this skill experience significant negative consequences. For example, friends may interpret their tardiness as a lack of caring, and employers assume a lack of commitment to their job.

Strategies for being punctual

- **Organise yourself.** This is one of those times when organisation and modelling are required. Plan ahead for timely departures and model this for your child.
- **No added extras.** Focus on getting yourself ready and monitoring your child. Resist the urge to sneak in the odd chore such as putting on a quick load of washing, or making a phone call.

- **Use launch pads.** This is an assigned spot in the house for items that will be required when you leave the house. Family launch pads can be a basket near the front door to be picked up as you leave the house. Individual launch pads can be a shelf in the bedroom for storing items such as wallets, keys, public transport tickets (e.g. SmartRiders), and whatever else needs to leave the house with your child. The schoolbag, packed the night before, is a great launch pad for school days.
- **Focus on the departure time, not the estimated arrival time.** Decide what time you need to leave home in order to arrive punctually, and make that time your only focus. When you focus on the arrival time it opens up all sorts of opportunities for debates about how long you 'really need to make it in time'.
- **Inform your child what time you will be leaving**, and set up a visual timer to show them how much time they have. Chunk the time into 15-minute sprints if necessary.
- **Provide a list of 'getting ready' instructions if necessary.** Use the timer and list to keep your child focused.

How can I teach my child to remember?

People with ADHD often have excellent long-term memories. However, they are also described as absent-minded. They tend to forget the steps required to complete activities, and can be disorganised in their thinking. These characteristics are caused by working-memory impairments. Accept this as part of ADHD and work with your child to design the necessary support systems.

Externalise working memory

As with time management, an effective way to support working memory is to make it visible by providing the information your child needs to complete tasks at the point of performance. Examples of externalising working memory include lists for morning and evening routines, dot points for assignments, launch pads and timers. Look for every opportunity to have a reminder for your child at the relevant time and place. Here are some more examples:

- Remind your child to use the homework diary by attaching a small distraction ribbon or material to their pencil-case zipper.
- Remind your child to remove electronics from the bedroom each night by wrapping an elastic band around their toothbrush.
- Remind your child to pack their school lunch each morning by sticking a post-it note on the cereal box.

Revamp your reminders

It is important to note that reminders will lose their effectiveness over time and simply become invisible to your child. When that happens, change them. For example, replace the distraction tool with a ribbon. Remember to record successful reminders in your child's DIY manual. They can be recycled at a later stage.

How can I teach my child to manage their 'stuff'?

An untidy environment creates an 'untidy mind'. ADHD brains need a tidy, organised environment in order to operate effectively. Don't be fooled by claims that they 'know where everything is'. Be guided, instead, by the amount of time your child spends looking for things they have misplaced. Find a balance between the level of tidiness they require, and the level of untidiness you can tolerate. Important points to remember include the following:

- **Design systems with your child's input.** Avoid being rigid about the type of system your child uses. If they have a say from the start they will be far more likely to work at making it stick.
- **Keep systems simple and visible.** If your child has to stop and remember where to put something, it will probably end up in the wrong place.

Bedroom stuff

Many bedrooms have a 'floordrobe', with a mix of clean and dirty clothes strewn across the carpet. Toys, books, games, hairdryers and other well-used items seem to find their way into piles of clutter and chaos. Work with your child to develop a simple system for bedroom stuff. The goal of your system should not be to have a pristine bedroom, but rather to make it easier for your child and family to function. Set achievable targets, avoiding overly high standards, at all times. Other strategies include the following:

- **Place a laundry basket in the bedroom.** If your child does not have to leave the room to sort dirty laundry, there is a better chance it will happen.
- **Design a simple system for clean clothes.** For example, include clearly marked shelves or drawers and plenty of empty coathangers.
- **Have clearly marked containers for toys, puzzles and games.** Tidying will be easier if everything has an obvious home.

- **Post a list of tidying instructions.** Simply telling your child to tidy their room could result in blank stares and a general feeling of being overwhelmed. Aside from providing a starting point and a focus for the task at the point of performance, the list also ensures that you both have the same expectations.
- **Teach your child to 'sweep'.** Once you have established the level of tidiness that works for you, teach your child to maintain it. Ideally you want them to put things away immediately, but they will have a tendency to slip. Develop the habit of a visual sweep – to identify items that are out of place and deal with them before things get out of hand.

Stuff that spreads

Children (and some adults) with ADHD are prone to littering the entire house with their belongings. This causes problems on two fronts. First, it adds to the clutter and encroaches on communal spaces. Second, it results in frequent family hunting expeditions for 'lost' items.

- **Have a basket for stuff that spreads.** Choose a place in the house to keep your child's 'spreadable' items safe and contained. Insist on it being emptied on a weekly basis.
- **Launch pads.** Have your child assign a spot in the house for items they will require when leaving the house: a shelf in the bedroom, schoolbag or other convenient space.

School stuff

As children progress through school, they gather more and more stuff. Some children with ADHD manage this well. Others manage to transform school supplies, books and notes from an ordered system to a chaotic mess. Uneaten school lunches congregate at the bottom of schoolbags, along with scrunched-up papers. Books required for homework are left in the school locker, and completed homework is left on the 'floordrobe'. Decide on some simple steps to help control this chaos. As always, involve your child in choosing and designing these systems.

- **Colour code each subject** and keep the same colours for core subjects every year if possible. That way, getting what is required for English, for example, will be as simple as grabbing the purple stuff. The less there is to remember at the point of performance, the easier it will be.
- **Streamline the schoolbag.** Avoid complicated filing systems, and opt for a system that is easy to implement 'on the run'. Some students choose a colour-coded notebook for each subject with a sleeve inside the cover for handouts. Others choose to have a single plastic pocket for all handouts that is carried to each class and brought home each day. Fewer steps result in higher success rates.
- **Simplify the workspace.** Consider using a pigeonhole system and assigning a pigeonhole for each subject in order to contain the paper that stays at home. Label it clearly or colour code it accordingly. While this may not be as ordered as a lever-arch filing system, it will enable your child to keep subject materials together with less effort and fewer steps.
- **Sort the locker.** Visit the school with your child (outside of school hours) to conquer the locker chaos. Colour code your child's timetable and stick a copy inside the locker door, with a moveable marker, such as a post-it note, to easily identify where they are in the week and day. This will make it easier to focus on checking that they have what they need and

where they are headed next. Conduct a locker cull at the end of every term, and help your child set it up again when the new term starts. Again, it is best to do this outside of school hours, to save your child embarrassment.

- **Have what they need, where they need it, when they need it.** Teach your child to spend some time each night packing the schoolbag for the next day, by checking the timetable and homework diary as part of their homework routine. Also, devise a reminder to help your child pause at their locker after every school day to run through what needs to be taken home.

How can I teach my child to be a friend?

Social interactions are often problematic for children with ADHD. Friends can be few and far between, and birthday party invitations can be rare. Some children are good at making friends, but have difficulty keeping them. The social skills that are easily assimilated by most children seem to bypass them. Tips to help your child be a better friend include the following:

- **Find friends among supportive families.** When you find your 'tribe' of other families dealing with ADHD you have opportunities for your children to socialise. While there is no guarantee that children with ADHD will get along well, your tribe will provide a supportive space for your child to learn social skills.
- **Encourage friendships with children from different age groups.** The emotional immaturity associated with ADHD means that children of the same age are not necessarily a good social fit. You may find that your child interacts successfully

with children who are younger, and display a similar level of maturity, or with children who are older, and are therefore more forgiving of social clumsiness.

- **Be your child's friend.** Organise social outings for you and your child and model the skills they need to learn in order to make friends. Give your child the opportunity to practise being a friend to you.

- **Set up successful 'play dates'.** Focus on inviting one friend at a time. Keep the encounters short, and leave both children wanting more time together. Structure the time to include an activity (such as Lego, trampolining, sailing or cooking) that will allow your child to show their best side while they are getting to know their friend.

How can I teach my child to limit screen time?

The digital age brings many positives.

- It helps to level the playing field for children with ADHD who may have difficulty transferring their thoughts onto paper.

- It provides a range of assistive technology for those with issues around reading and writing. Voice-to-text software and mind-mapping software, for example, are helpful for many.

- Many schools are moving towards making learning and assessment materials available online for parents and students, thus reducing the frustration around forgetting things at home or school.

- Social media can also provide a useful socialising tool for some. Just as the previous generation of teenagers were chided for spending too much time on the family telephone, today's 'digital natives' spend time talking on Skype or using instant messaging platforms to communicate with their peers.

However, technology becomes problematic because it is so seamless. For modern-day parents it is not as simple as requesting that their child hang up and get on with their homework. Today's students are completing their homework on the same device that they use to play games and to socialise. The executive-function impairments associated with ADHD can cause students to open a website with the intention of staying there for a minute but becoming absorbed for much longer than anticipated.

What can parents do to reduce time spent on screens?

- **Have clear guidelines and agreements** in place with your children and be consistent about enforcing them. Include the whole family when deciding on screen usage so that everybody is clear about the rules.
- **Organise regular family activities that do not include screens.** Compile a list of activities that you can do together instead, such as board-game evenings and reading. Remember to include outdoors activities, such as hikes and picnics.
- **Lead by example.** Make a commitment to putting your smartphone away in the evenings. If your children see you checking your emails or social network sites regularly, they will be less inclined to monitor their usage of screens.
- **Encourage your child to monitor their own screen usage.** Encourage them to install software to prevent them from visiting certain sites during homework activities. Have your child compile a list of fun activities that do not require screens.

- **Have screen-free time as a family** and observe these times routinely. For example, no screen at meal times, no screens on Sunday mornings.

- **Manage transitions from screen time** and teach your child to do the same. Remember that it will be difficult for your child to switch their attention from the highly stimulating screen-related activity to something less exciting. Agree on a system that includes a warning, with a visual timer, and use it each time you need your child to make the transition.

- **Remove electronic devices at bedtime**, and return them in the morning when your child is ready for school. Midnight socialising via apps such as Facebook or Skype is more common than you would imagine and it hampers healthy sleep routines. Also, access to screens in the morning is a distraction when children are meant to be getting ready for school.

- **Is gaming the only thing your child feels good about?** If so, work with your child to identify other activities where they can do well.

- **Is there an addiction?** Seek expert advice from your child's doctor if you are concerned.

Chapter 6

What will help my child at school?

Terry's story

Before I was diagnosed with ADHD, school was really hard. I had difficulties getting organised at home, even getting ready for school in the morning was a struggle, my grades at school were lower than I expected them to be and I was not confident socially. Starting medication was the first step. My grades improved but it didn't solve everything. For starters, I was struggling to write essays, and losing focus in maths tests. And I was still disorganised. My assignments were happening at the last minute, and I kept losing stuff I needed.

Coaching helped me design routines in a way that suited me. I started using the 30/30 app in the mornings, instead of posting a list on the fridge. I learned how to break assignments down and plan them with the help of a wall calendar and weekly planner. Maths tests became easier when I separated number questions from word-based tasks. But writing essays was still a huge problem, even though I was getting a lot of help at school. My mum took me for more testing, and I was diagnosed with dyslexia and dysgraphia on top of the ADHD. Although that might sound bad, it was actually a good thing to know, because I qualified for more support at school. I use a computer for all written assessments now. And now that I understand what helps me learn, I know what help to ask for at school.

At the start of year 11, the teachers gave us a talk about how we all needed to be on top of our work for the last 2 years of school. When I saw my mates panic, I realised that I was better prepared for the challenge than anyone else in the class. It was a great feeling. There is a lot of work, but I'm managing to get it done. I still have bad patches, but my confidence has grown, and I'm really proud of myself.

What are the challenges?

School can be particularly challenging for children with ADHD. Parents need a clear understanding of the difficulties their children face at school in order to describe them to teachers and to request meaningful support.

- Symptoms of ADHD, associated executive-function impairments and added learning difficulties make it harder for them to learn.
- Children with ADHD vary in the type of symptoms they display (dreamy or hyperactive, or both). Also, their behaviours can vary throughout the day and across different learning contexts. This inconsistency is sometimes interpreted by teachers and others as laziness or a lack of effort.
- Social interactions can be problematic.
- They experience great difficulties with organisation and time management.

- Transitions between activities, between classrooms and between environments (such as the playground and classroom) will take longer and need to be managed.

Preschool

During preschool, children learn important social, behavioural and academic skills essential for their future schooling. ADHD makes it harder for them to focus on teachers and participate in classroom activities and play. They struggle to follow classroom rules, stay on the mat, and to control inappropriate behaviours, such as throwing toys, fidgeting or talking. They find it difficult to self-regulate, especially if they also have anxiety.

Primary school

Behaviours expected in primary school do not come naturally to children with ADHD. They may struggle to sit still at a table and be quiet for long periods. It can be hard for them to pay attention, and to complete multistep tasks. Friends become important to them but due to poor social skills and lack of insight, maintaining friendships can be challenging. Consistent scaffolding will be required in order for them to learn how to work independently.

High school

When children with ADHD move to high school, they are faced with different environments, routines and expectations. Leaving behind the security of one main teacher and classroom, they change classrooms several times each day, and engage with many different teachers. They often find themselves arriving in class unprepared and without the necessary materials. Homework requirements increase to include larger projects assigned over long periods of time. As a result of poor organisation and time management, they often leave their assignments or test revision to the last minute, find themselves without the required resources to complete the work, and miss due dates. Friendships may become more challenging as they may lack insight into some of their behaviours which can be detrimental to new relationships.

How do I choose a school?

Parents often set out to find the best school for children with ADHD. What they should be doing is finding the best school for their *own child* with ADHD. Ideally, your child's school should cater for their challenges *and* provide opportunities for them to display their strengths or engage in activities of high interest. Consider the following when choosing a school:

- **Enquire about the level of knowledge** among *all* teachers in the school when it comes to ADHD. Having one or two specialist teachers is insufficient, unless they are educating and upskilling all staff on a regular basis.
- **Find out what supports exist in the school**, and whether they will be made available to your child. Specialist remedial programs, for example, may have criteria for inclusion and your child might not qualify.
- **Investigate specialist programs.** If your child has a special interest or talent in a particular field such as sport, drama, music or robotics, target schools with strong programs in those areas. School will become more engaging on the whole if it includes an area where they can engage or succeed. Once again, check inclusion criteria.
- **Factor in the 'community' effect** when deciding about the locality of your child's school. Will your child feel isolated

from their neighbourhood peers if they do not attend the local school? Will they be included with their class peers if they live some distance from school? Will it be beneficial to have two separate sets of friends?

- **Spend your money wisely.** There are excellent private schools and excellent public schools.
- **Homeschooling.** This is not common but may be the best option for children with multiple issues associated with their ADHD. High levels of uncontrolled social anxiety may make this option a wise decision for your child.

How can I inform the school and ask for support?

Some parents choose not to disclose their child's diagnosis to the school. While they may have valid concerns about how the school will respond, an ideal situation would be for the school to be well informed, and willing to support children with ADHD.

- **Provide the school with copies of reports** from professionals who have worked with your child. Ask the school to communicate with professionals who might be able to assist them to understand and meet your child's needs.
- **Provide information about ADHD and coexisting conditions** relevant to your child.
- **Provide information about 'twice-exceptional' children** if that applies to your child. For example, a student with ADHD in a robotics program may excel at some aspects of projects but fall short on others, such as report writing. Request that accommodations be provided when required.
- **Request and suggest strategies to assist your child at school.** See Twenty Tips for Teachers on page 148.

How should I communicate with the school and teachers?

Although most parents provide the school with information concerning their child's ADHD diagnosis, their communication is often with the principal or deputy principal, and it is assumed that the information will be passed on to all teachers. ADHD is an invisible condition, and your child's teacher, if uninformed, may not be aware that your child is struggling. Suggestions for improving communication include the following:

- **Give each teacher a page of information about your child.** Remember to include information about your child's strengths, not just the challenges they may experience. Include information about strategies you are working on at home to promote teamwork. Alert them to strategies successfully used by past teachers. Inform them also of strategies that have not been successful.

- **Ask teachers to communicate with you on a regular basis.** Such communication can occur through your child's diary or via email. This will allow you to inform teachers about challenges on the home front that could affect your child's performance at school from time to time. Similarly, the teachers can pass on information about problems encountered, or goals achieved by your child. In addition, ask teachers to inform you when projects and tests are assigned. This will allow you to work on time management and chunking skills with your child.

- **Develop a partnership with your child's teacher.** All too often battle lines are drawn between teachers and parents, and your child has nothing to gain from this dynamic. The teacher is the expert on teaching, and you are the expert on your child. Respectfully offer information on ADHD and other conditions that affect your child, and ask how you can work together. Remember to acknowledge the teacher's efforts.

- **Prepare for school meetings.** If you have requested the meeting, make a note of points you wish to discuss. For meetings requested by the teacher or school, ask about the purpose of the meeting and request names of attendees. If you feel intimidated, or if you become emotional in meetings, take your partner, a friend or advocate along for support. Offer to work with the school to identify and address challenges. Ask the school what they have in place to support your child, and what they are willing to add or modify.

How can I help my child learn?

We all learn differently. Children with ADHD learn very differently, but they are educated in a school system that teaches to the average learner. Make your child aware of different learning styles and encourage them to experiment in order to discover their own. This will make it easier for them to navigate the education system. Resist the urge to pigeonhole your child as one type of learner. Rather, let your child know that different learning situations will require different learning styles and they will have several that work well for them. Encourage them to record these in their DIY manual.

- **Auditory learners** like to hear information. Encourage them to record their notes onto a voice memo and listen to them whenever they can. Downloading podcasts for further information will also help them.

- **Verbal learners** like to talk in order to formulate ideas and remember information. Encourage them to 'teach' you about the work they have learned, or to record it. Voice-to-text-software can be very helpful in capturing their ideas. Be patient and allow them to 'ramble' until they get to the point if you are having a discussion.
- **Kinaesthetic learners** like to move in order to focus and understand. Fidgeting helps them to focus. When you tell a child with ADHD to stop fidgeting, you may be shutting their brain down, as they focus their attention on sitting still. Instead, teach them to fidget discreetly. Small fidget toys can be stored in the pencil case. Doodling is effective for some. Encourage them to move when they are working or studying at home, by sitting on a 'FitBall' or pacing while they listen to a podcast or watch a webinar.
- **Visual learners** like pictures in order to understand and remember information. These can be in the form of mind maps, charts, images and diagrams. Colour is very useful.
- **Global learners** like to get an overview of the information being conveyed with all the pieces clearly identified. Help them to place what they need to learn within the context of the bigger picture.
- **Sequential learners** like information in linear steps, with each step following logically from the previous one. Help them to identify those steps.

How can I teach my child to be a self-advocate?

Ideally, you want your child to learn to ask for assistance and accommodations. This skill will take some time for your child to master. It requires confidence, assertiveness, and, most importantly, it requires your child to have a good understanding of what helps them. All too often when children tell teachers that they don't understand something, teachers explain the information again in the same way that it was taught before. This may not help your child at all, and may also prevent them from seeking assistance in the future. How can you support your child to become an effective self-advocate?

- **Help them identify what help they need.** Teachers are always willing to offer support, but are often not aware of the best way to support children who learn differently. When your child has a clear understanding of what causes their challenges, and has experimented with some learning styles and specific strategies, they can start to identify helpful accommodations for specific teachers and subjects.
- **Teach them to articulate their requests clearly and assertively.** Have them rehearse their conversations with you until they are sufficiently confident to have them with their teacher. For example: '*Ms D, I find it really hard to listen and take notes at the same time in class. Would it be possible to get some brief notes from you on each topic, or have an arrangement to photocopy someone else's notes at lunchtime, or photograph the whiteboard at the end of each class?*'

How can I establish healthy homework and study routines?

Most ADHD families would agree that homework is a significant source of frustration, discord and conflict in the home. To complicate matters, your child could be experiencing 'rebound' from their medication wearing off, or their medication could have worn off altogether by the time they sit down to work. There is also a good chance that your child could be fatigued from the extra mental effort required to concentrate in class all day.

Homework considerations

Effective homework routines require organisation, consistency and calm.

- Enlist homework help in the form of a mentor or tutor if it is affecting your relationship with your child.
- Homework is your child's responsibility. Support them to take that responsibility.
- Consequences for unfinished homework are the school's responsibility. Clarify those consequences in advance.
- Advocate for your child and request accommodations if homework expectations are unrealistic.

Helpful homework habits

- Find a 'homework diary' system that suits your child. This could be a paper diary, a homework app, or the school portal.
- Plan a regular homework timeslot. After-school activities might prevent it from happening at the same time each day, so you may need two regular timeslots.
- Allow some free time between school and homework, but avoid screens.
- Give your child a 10-minute warning leading up to the homework timeslot and develop a transition routine. For example, have them complete what they are doing during that period, wash their hands and get a drink or snack.

- Separate the set-up from the task. Have everything required at hand to avoid distractions down the track.
- Create 'sprints' by chunking the homework into short time-slots. Use a timer to make these slots visible.
- Encourage revision or reading if there is no assigned homework.
- Pack away immediately once finished, and pack the schoolbag for the next day.
- Allow a 'reward' after homework in the form of an activity your child loves.

In preschool and primary school

- Describe the homework challenges to the teacher; they normally only see your child medicated and refreshed, and may be unaware of your struggles.
- Clarify realistic homework expectations with the teacher and request some flexibility, such as stopping after an assigned time regardless of output.
- Provide the teacher with regular feedback concerning homework.

In high school
Complete the steps below with your child until they have learned the skills for themselves. This may take some time.

- Consult the diary every day – even if there is no homework.
- Add long-term dates to the wall calendar, and cross off each day that passes – this will make time and tasks visible.
- Dot-point projects as soon as they are assigned. This will clarify requirements and identify potential obstacles upfront.

It will also create chunks, which provide an entry for your child to get started.

- Use weekly planners to identify homework and assignment opportunities.
- Encourage your child to go over notes from class each night to consolidate what they have learned.

How can my child get accommodations for exams and assessments?

Students with ADHD are entitled to accommodation in their final school exams, particularly when a coexisting condition further affects their performance. While some schools are proactive in setting up accommodations for their students, other school are less conscientious and parents must take the lead.

- **Investigate possible accommodations for your child.** Australian national guidelines have been developed by the Australasian Curriculum Assessment Certification Authorities (ACACA). Possible accommodations include rest breaks for students with ADHD, extra time to work for students with specific learning disorders and the use of a computer for students with a specific learning disorder – with impairment in written expression (also known as dysgraphia).
- **Arrange relevant testing** to support your application. Specific psychometric testing is required at specific times by the curriculum authorities. The psychologist at your child's school can advise you in this regard. Alternatively, contact the curriculum authority in your state for clarification.

- **Have accommodations in place as early as possible.** Evidence of case management by the school is regarded as essential by the curriculum authorities. This should confirm the problems experienced by the student in written examinations, outline the accommodations provided during school examinations and comment on the effect of these arrangements on the student's achievement.
- **Advocate for your child and ask the school to do the same.** If your application is turned down, you are entitled to an appeal, which would be strengthened by the support of the school.

What about technology and apps?

While the digital age has created problems with over-reliance on screens for some (see 'Is electronic addiction a problem?' on page 37), it has also provided us with the means to support ADHD-related impairments, and to level the playing field for students with ADHD or specific learning disorders.

Assistive technology

The executive-function impairments often associated with ADHD can cause challenges in learning environments. For example, many students with ADHD struggle to translate their thoughts and ideas into the written word. The physical act of writing with a pen can exacerbate this, as they switch focus between formulating ideas and forming letters on the page. Similarly, students may struggle with note taking in class, losing focus as they switch between listening and writing.

- **Computers** enable students to 'dump' their ideas without focusing on neatness, spelling and structure on the first pass. They are then able to revisit and edit the text into the format required. For many students, typing on a computer is a more fluid writing process than using pen and paper.
- **Touch-typing** can streamline this process even more. There are several interactive, engaging programs available for learning this skill.
- **Voice-to-text software** allows students to speak their ideas (into a headset microphone) which are then converted to text. Most smartphones include this feature, which is ideal for recording ideas 'on the run'.
- **Text-to-voice software** enables students to have written text read aloud to them. Some computers have this as a built-in function, or the software can be downloaded. It is valuable for struggling readers, and is also a good study tool.
- **Recording devices for note taking** include pens that allow simultaneous recording/speaking and writing. With permission, students can record a class or lecture while writing notes with the pen, which then syncs the recording to the written notes. Some tablet applications perform similar functions.
- **Apps** can help with the executive-function-related challenges around studying, organisation and time management. Many students have smartphones and/or tablets, which include some of the useful functions listed below.
  - **Time-tracking apps** help students to keep their activities on track by providing visual and audio time prompts. They make time visible and audible.
  - **Calendars** provide a picture of the student's time, enabling them to assign tasks to particular periods and keep track of

commitments. Reminders can be set to ensure deadlines are not forgotten.

– **Task managers** provide a format for students to 'chunk' their work and keep track of their progress towards the completed task.

– **Internet-usage control apps** can be programmed to block/allow access to certain internet sites at various times of the day.

– **Apps for generating white noise and ambient sounds** can be useful for blocking audible distractions, making it easier for students to focus on homework and study.

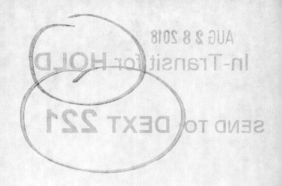

Chapter 7

How can teachers and schools support students with ADHD?

What are the typical challenges for students with ADHD?

While much information about ADHD centres on the core symptoms of inattention, hyperactivity and impulsivity, it is also helpful to focus on the executive-function impairments typical of the disorder which have serious implications in the classroom for children with ADHD. Although the impairments may seem trivial to most, they create significant difficulties for people with ADHD that can persist across their lifetime. Teachers may find themselves frustrated if they do not have a clear understanding of the associated behaviours. (See 'What is executive functioning?' page 32.) In summary, executive-functioning impairments show up for students as:

- the inability to pause, self-regulate, filter out distractions and draw on skills or knowledge required at the point of performance
- time blindness, which prevents them from planning towards extended deadlines
- impaired hindsight and foresight, resulting in 'mistakes' being repeated despite consequences
- impaired working memory that is easily overloaded, resulting in information blanks
- the inability to self-motivate, requiring immediate consequences and rewards as incentives
- difficulty controlling emotions, resulting in angry outbursts, ruminating or mental meltdowns
- the inability to plan and problem-solve when faced with challenging tasks.

While anyone can have occasional impairments in their executive function, people with ADHD experience much more difficulty in the development and use of these functions than do most others of the same age and developmental level. However, even those with severe ADHD often have some activities where their executive function works very well. This makes it hard for people to accept their challenges in other domains.

Students with ADHD often have coexisting mental health conditions, behavioural disorders or learning difficulties, which further impact their abilities at school.

Challenges experienced by students with ADHD at specific stages of schooling are described in Chapter 6 on page 103.

How can the school support students with ADHD?

The debilitating effects of ADHD are most apparent in the school setting, where children exhibit difficulty learning, sustaining attention, socialising and maintaining appropriate levels of activity. These deficits often result in academic underachievement, suspension, expulsion, and failure to complete schooling. Schools can help in the following ways:

- **Provide professional development for teachers.** ADHD is a serious disorder. It is also a treatable disorder. Ensure that teachers are provided with opportunities to learn the skills required to engage and support this vulnerable group of students.

- **Enable smooth transitions.** Allow additional orientation for new students with ADHD who may need more time than their peers to familiarise themselves with their new surroundings. Encourage parents to bring their children to the school before the term starts, to identify classrooms, the canteen and toilets, and to practise using their locker.

- **Have clear lines of communication for parents.** Communication between parents and teachers in primary school is generally straightforward. However, high school poses challenges for parents who need teachers to be aware of their child's challenges, whether ongoing or suddenly exacerbated by an incident outside of school. Parents need to know who they can talk to, and they need to be confident that the information will be passed on.

- **Share information with all teachers.** Parents sometimes provide schools with comprehensive information, only to find that it is not circulated to all teachers who have contact with their child. Have a system that makes important information available to relevant staff.

119

- **Inform relief teachers.** Students with ADHD may find it particularly challenging when their regular teacher is away. Established routines may be disrupted, and behaviours can escalate or be misinterpreted by a teacher who is uninformed. Strategies for specific students can make life easier for the student and teacher.

- **Take a team approach.** Although it is often trivialised, ADHD is a complex condition, commonly co-occurring with separate learning disabilities, behavioural disorders and mental health issues such as anxiety or depression. Seek input from the student's treating team and provide them with feedback.

- **Suspend judgement.** Due to the highly heritable nature of the disorder, there is often more than one family member diagnosed with ADHD. And it is not uncommon for a parent to have similar challenges. While it is not the school's responsibility to manage forgetful, disorganised parents, some simple measures can lighten their load and minimise frustration for all concerned. Send notifications electronically and have information available on the school website portal. Some schools have an app as part of the school calendar of events that sends out automated text message reminders.

- **Compassion for families.** Families affected by ADHD do it tough. There are higher levels of separation and divorce, depression in parents, sibling conflict and social isolation. Children are rejected in the playground, and parents are judged in the carpark. Make your school an ADHD safe place.

- **Maintain the school website.** In theory, all schools have a portal, where teachers share resources, assignment notifications, marking rubrics and other information. In practice, the school portal is used consistently and effectively by some schools, and sporadically by others. A well-maintained school portal levels the playing field for students with executive-function impairments, as it provides them with the information they need to complete homework at the point of performance. Ensure that your school portal is supporting your students in this way.

- **Have a clear medication policy.** With the introduction of long-acting medications, fewer children require medication doses during the school day. However, for various reasons, many schools still have medication on-site for students. There is considerable stigma associated with ADHD medications. Your students will benefit from a system that allows them to discreetly and privately take their medication at school if needed.

- **Facilitate assessment accommodations.** Students with ADHD are entitled to modified assessment and examination conditions. In order to have these measures in place for students' final school exams, exam boards require evidence of case management over time. The process is complicated and confusing for parents. Identify and implement accommodations for students with ADHD, and then advocate on their behalf to ensure that they have a fair outcome for their final exams.

- **Designate safe zones.** Mental meltdowns occur for some students with ADHD due to their impaired ability to control emotions. They may take the form of angry outbursts, or extreme anxiety or rumination. Have a timeout system for students which allows them to leave the classroom if they feel upset and go straight to a designated safe place in the school to work through the strong emotions with a staff member.

How can teachers support students with ADHD in the classroom?

ADHD is the most commonly diagnosed mental health condition in childhood. It is also the most misunderstood, and is often referred to as an 'invisible disability'. As a teacher, you can do the following:

- **Educate yourself about ADHD.** Regular professional development in this area is important. Once teachers understand the challenges, they are able to design and implement strategies to improve outcomes for students with ADHD.
- **Get the full picture.** Children with ADHD vary in the type of symptoms they display (inattentive or hyperactive, or both). Each will have unique challenges that are often complicated by coexisting conditions. They will also have strengths but may struggle to show them. Find out what is going on for each student with ADHD. Parents are always a good source of information, as are reports from doctors and other professionals.
- **Level the playing field.** Provide support as required. Allow the use of computers in class for students who have difficulties with writing. Organise audio books for students who struggle to read. Provide summarised notes if copying from the board is a challenge, and allow students to photograph the whiteboard or other visuals at the end of a lesson. Make worksheets available in an electronic format if students are prone to losing handouts.
- **Maintain confidentiality and respect.** Because of the stigma associated with ADHD, students tend not to disclose their diagnosis. Let them know that you understand their

122

challenges and that you will not share information about them with other students or parents. Support them discreetly in the classroom wherever possible. Try to avoid calling their name repeatedly. Instead, have agreed-upon strategies and signals that are understood by you and the student in order to assist focus. Never mention medication in the classroom or in front of others. Avoid shaming students for bad behaviour. Each time a teacher shows disrespect towards a student, they are giving fellow students permission to do the same.

- **Allow students to fidget and move.** There is some evidence to suggest that students with ADHD focus better when they are moving or fidgeting. With that in mind, be tolerant of fidgeting that is not distracting other students. Encourage students to fidget discreetly. Doodling is a great fidgeting strategy, as is playing with a small piece of Blu Tack, or rubbing a small pebble. Have an agreement that students may leave the room for a bathroom break if they become restless.

- **Engage students to prevent challenging behaviours.** Research indicates that students with ADHD are more likely to misbehave in class if they do not have a grasp on the material being presented. Consider providing alternative ways for students to present their learning in assignments, such as in the form of a movie, audio presentation or website. By making the curriculum accessible to students you will reduce their off-task behaviours considerably.

- **Help students deal with inconsistency.** The behaviours and abilities of students with ADHD can vary from day to day, or throughout the day and across different learning contexts. This inconsistency, which can occur even when students are medicated, is sometimes interpreted as laziness or a lack of effort. It is frustrating for teachers when students may be capable of a task one day, but not the next. It is even more frustrating for the students themselves. Avoid comments such as: 'Why couldn't you do this yesterday?' or 'You did this yesterday. Why can't you do it today?' Instead, celebrate good days unconditionally. When they have a bad day, remind them of their good days as proof that there will be more.

- **Find their buried treasures.** While your students with ADHD may have gaps in their abilities, they will certainly have islands of competence, or even excellence. Provide opportunities for them to showcase their strengths. Facilitate groups that allow them to make meaningful contributions. For example, if your student is a great inventor but a poor writer, pair them with a talented scribe.

- **Teach students to sprint.** ADHD brains are great sprinters. They are able to work towards deadlines that are close in time, but lose sight of deadlines that are further out. If they can see a finish line, they are more likely to get started on a task. Help students create sprints by setting a 10/20/30-minute timer, and have them complete as much work as possible in that time. Along with sprints, frequent short breaks can be extremely effective. Allow your student to create a cycle of timed sprints and timed breaks to get through a large task.

- **Devise transition routines.** Executive-function impairments make it difficult for students to switch between tasks and environments. Be flexible about transitions between tasks. If a student who has taken longer to get started on an activity is focused when it is time to move on, consider allowing them extra time to complete it. Design a routine for settling into classroom activities and make it visible at the point of performance. Primary school students can have it pasted onto their desks. High school students can have it written on a computer desktop sticky note or the front of their homework diary.

- **Teach students to brain dump.** When they find themselves focused, students are often reluctant to stop working, knowing how hard it will be to get started again. If at all possible, leave a focused student to complete a task. However, if work must stop, have students write down the next steps of the task. When they return, those notes will provide their next entry point.

- **Dot-point tasks.** Because of their inability to break work into small steps, students become overwhelmed by what they perceive to be an enormous task. In the classroom, giving students one task at a time or a short list of dot points creates an entry point, making it easier to get started. Long-term assignments and projects should also be broken down into chunks and dot points.

- **Create shorter deadlines.** Assign portions of assignments and have students discuss these with you regularly. Aside from the discussed benefits of chunking, this prevents students from over-focusing on one aspect of the assignment to the detriment of others.

- **Provide written instructions at the point of performance.** Students with ADHD are unable to remember lists of verbal instructions. Write instructions for classroom tasks on the whiteboard, or provide worksheets. Ensure that homework is clearly described and presented, and the instructions are uploaded to the school portal or emailed to students.

- **Make time visible.** The ADHD brain does not have an internal clock. In order to understand time, your student needs to see it. Time will appear to drag on endlessly when tasks are challenging. Use visual timers to illustrate the end point of a challenging task. Many projects are completed at the last minute as students lose sight of deadlines that seem far in the future. Have a planner on display with assignment due dates clearly marked, and cross off each day as it passes to give students a reference point. This creates a picture of the time available to them to complete a task.

- **Encourage 'free-writing'.** Sometimes the best ideas get lost as students struggle to articulate them in an appropriate format or style. If this is the case, encourage students to get their ideas onto a page first and then arrange them into the appropriate format. This works best on a computer. For example, students might write the body of an essay first, and then go back to writing the introduction.

- **Use white noise.** Allow students to listen to music, ambient sounds or white noise through earphones while working independently. For many students this is an effective way to block out external and internal distractions. Not only will it increase their focus on the task at hand, it will also prevent them from distracting others.

- **Manage meltdowns.** The impaired ability to control emotions results in students with ADHD experiencing sudden floods of emotion. This comes on swiftly and persists for some time. For some students it manifests as angry outbursts, while others internalise unpleasant thoughts. Have a timeout system for students that allows them to leave the classroom if they feel upset and go straight to a designated safe place in the school to work through the strong emotions.

- **Be flexible about homework requirements.** Homework turns homes into battlefields for families dealing with ADHD. While many students with ADHD will have the benefit of medication during school hours to help them focus, this is generally not the case during the homework period. Many experience a period of restless 'rebound' while their medication is wearing off, and mental fatigue is common.

- **Partner with parents.** Maintain regular communication. This can be done either via a communications book, particularly in primary school, or via email for students in high school. Do inform parents as soon as assignments or long-term projects are set. Students with ADHD require extensive scaffolding by parents in order to have projects completed on time. Awareness of due dates enables parents to put plans in place in a timely manner. Remember to share students' successes as well as their challenges, as parents are too often bombarded with complaints from the school.

Chapter 8

How can I help my child transition to adulthood?

Michael's story

Michael was a hyperactive risk-taker from the day he was born. He was running at 10 months, sometimes straight off the top step into thin air. In primary school he tried to 'plug' his Lego creations into the power sockets. In high school he was mad about skating – not at those lovely skate parks the council so thoughtfully provides for young people, but in the streets and parks of the city, where there were steps, ledges and walls to launch off. I was sure he would be seriously injured. But he never was.

He was a bright boy, but underachieving at school. And the education system failed him badly. Because he was struggling to pass English, they refused to let him study physics and chemistry. He left year 12 with a really bad score, and I worried that he would struggle to get any sort of qualification. But he took himself off to Adult College and completed high school physics and chemistry in a year with distinction. Then he enrolled at the state's top university and completed an engineering degree with honours. English may be problematic, but maths and physics are effortless. Along the way he started driving, and despite the scary research on ADHD drivers, he has never had a single demerit point. And despite the scary research on ADHD relationships, he is engaged to the love of his life.

How did this happen? With a lot of hard work by Michael, and his determination that he would and could achieve more than the school system predicted. With support from pivotal teachers and lecturers along the way who recognised his intelligence, and saw his learning difficulties for what they are — not laziness or a lack of motivation. With a group of friends who saw his good heart and stuck by him through thick and thin. With the presence of wonderful doctors who found the right medications to focus that beautiful brain. And with his family by his side, learning from our mistakes and finding better strategies together. It took him a little longer to get there. But get there he did.

Parenting a child with ADHD can be an anxiety-provoking process. Part of supporting your child is believing that they can and will be successful in life with the right support. If you find yourself worrying about possible pitfalls in 10 years' time, remind yourself that your child will have a further 10 years of education and support behind them by then, and avoid projecting their current maturity or skill set onto their future lives. When your child sees you having confidence in them, it is easier for them to feel confident about their future.

As children leave school to embark on their young adult lives, they are entering a period of great transition. New environments require new skill sets, or the modification of existing skill sets. Some support systems and structures, such as those found in the school environment, are no longer present. In addition, they are required to make the transition to adult medical services, leaving the 'safety' of a paediatrician they may have known for some time. There are many things that parents can do, however, to prevent their child from becoming 'lost in transition'.

How can I build a village?

We have all heard the saying: 'It takes a village to raise a child'. When your child has ADHD it may be harder to find that village, but it is even more important. As your child makes the transition into the adult world, they may not have acquired all the skills they need. However, they may want their parents to be less involved in their lives. It is important for your child to have a group of trusted adults to call on. In addition to the treating professionals and support staff discussed in this chapter, consider the following potential village members:

- **Family members or family friends.** Encourage your child to build strong relationships with trusted adults in their lives. They may need someone, other than a parent, to talk to at times.
- **ADHD coaches.** ADHD coaches work with clients to identify areas where skills need to be learned or improved. They also provide valuable education about ADHD and how it affects individual clients. Strategies are then tailored for each client and each situation. As coaching is not a regulated industry, always check out their credentials (granted by the International Coach Federation), as well as the level of ADHD specialisation (e.g. Professional Association of ADHD Coaches accreditation) when hiring an ADHD coach.

- **Psychologists.** ADHD is often characterised by strong emotions. Psychologists are able to help develop strategies to manage them. In addition, they help treat coexisting disorders such as depression and anxiety.
- **Mentors.** Encourage your child to seek out mentors. These can be found in formal mentoring programs, such as those in tertiary institutions and in the workplace. They can also be informal relationships. For example, an experienced co-worker may agree to support them at work, or an older student may offer them study support and guidance. Your child can also benefit greatly from serving as a mentor for someone else.
- **Support groups.** These come in various forms. If young people feel uncomfortable sitting around a table talking about ADHD or themselves, they may find the anonymity of social media support groups more suitable.

How can I smooth the transition to adult medical services?

The treatment of ADHD in adults is the domain of psychiatrists. While paediatricians have the ability to hold onto their patients with ADHD up to the age of 25 in Australia, at some stage your child will need to transfer to a psychiatrist. The general consensus is that transition occurs around 18 years when your child has completed their schooling.

- **Be guided by your child's paediatrician through this process.** They know your child's needs and are well placed to recommend an adult specialist. In addition, they will forward your child's medical records to their new specialist.

131

- **Set up a reminder system.** Your young adult will need to keep track of prescription repeats and appointment dates. Scaffold and support them through this process until they have it under control.
- **Encourage your child to develop a relationship with a single GP.** A GP can function as a consistent checkpoint for the young adult in the health system. In addition, GPs are able to co-prescribe medication for adults with ADHD, if authorised by the treating specialist.
- **Encourage the use of a single pharmacist.** Government regulations require prescriptions for stimulant medications to remain with the pharmacist, so there is already a regular point of contact for your child. Encourage them to consolidate that contact by leaving any other prescriptions with the same pharmacist.

How can I smooth the transition to tertiary study?

The move from school to the tertiary sector sees students transition from a highly structured to a relatively unstructured environment. While this can be liberating at first, the novelty soon wears off as the work builds up. Students often become overwhelmed and feel tempted to withdraw. But there is much that can be done to keep them studying successfully:

- **Encourage them to register with Disability Services.** The support they receive in the tertiary sector can make all the difference to their academic future. Students with ADHD find the tertiary sector far more accommodating than school. Depending on their specific challenges, and on the recommendation of their treating specialist, they are afforded accommodations which may include extra time to work in exams, flexibility around assignment deadlines and access to assistive technology such as computers and voice-to-text software. Registration with Disability Services is confidential and is never reflected on their academic record. In addition, Tertiary Disability Services advocate on behalf of students, and teach them the skills required for self-advocacy. They are often located in the same building as the university or TAFE health centres which provide government-funded counselling and medical consultations for students in a convenient and non-threatening setting.

- **Encourage them to be flexible.** Although the tertiary sector does not provide the same level of routine, structure and accountability as the school system, it creates much more flexibility. For example, attendance at university lectures is not compulsory, and most institutions provide lecture recordings within hours of the live event. Students attending TAFE may request permission to record lectures. This allows students who find it hard to concentrate in large, noisy rooms to watch recorded lectures at a later date in a quiet environment, and to pause whenever they wish. Students are also better able to make use of their best study windows as they can nominate their preferred tutorial slots on their timetable. Flexibility around assignment delivery at university and TAFE reduces stress at times of heavy workload.

- **Encourage them to create their own structure.** Although flexibility in the tertiary sector affords students opportunities to modify study habits, it is essential for them to create their own structures in order to give themselves the best chance of success. Routines and calendars which make their time and deadlines visible will allow them to be realistic about their study and social commitments. Regular exercise and healthy sleep routines are also important. If help is required, encourage your child to contact student services or to hire an ADHD coach.

- **Encourage them to 'ease themselves in' if necessary.** Students with ADHD are 'time-poor'. It often takes them longer to complete assignments and studies than their non-ADHD peers. Some students find it helpful to reduce their study load and spread their degree over a longer time period.

How can I smooth the transition to full-time employment?

With the odd exception, there is no place for parental input at your child's or young adult's workplace. However, parents can operate as valuable sounding boards as their children encounter challenges at work. Young adults can be empowered by the process of brainstorming solutions with their parents and rehearsing conversations or scenarios before they take place.

- **Encourage self-advocacy.** Ensure that your child is aware of their strengths as well as their challenges. Help them to identify the aspects of their work that they do well and modifications or supports they could request in order to improve their performance.
- **Name the symptom, not the condition.** If your child needs to disclose their ADHD diagnosis, the Human Resources Department is the appropriate place to do so. Beyond that, support can be requested by describing the characteristics of ADHD. For example: 'I need to write those instructions down as I have a bad memory at times'.

What can be helpful to manage ADHD in adolescence and adulthood?

Many of the strategies suggested in previous chapters are useful for all ages. In addition, try the following:

- Use a smartphone with alarms to remind you of appointments, items on your to-do list, taking medication and to set work reminders.
- Have a notepad available in your car, by your bedside and on the kitchen bench so that you can write down important thoughts.
- Plan the day ahead of time so that everything is well organised.
- Use a smart device on your keys and wallet so they are easy to locate.
- Split larger tasks into smaller, more doable tasks which may be easier to manage.
- If tasks are too detailed, uninteresting or tedious, look at ways that they may be achieved by either doing them with someone else or rewarding yourself when they are completed.
- Make healthy eating choices.
- Exercise regularly, especially outdoors, and enjoy nature.
- Keep on top of your chores.
- Reduce clutter in your home and room.
- Keep your regular appointments with your doctor and other professionals, including your psychologist, occupational therapist or ADHD coach.

Chapter 9

Myths and tips about ADHD

Twenty myths about ADHD

Myth 1: ADHD is only diagnosed in developed countries
ADHD is diagnosed all around the world, in approximately 3–8 per cent of children under 18 years and 3–4 per cent of adults.

Myth 2: ADHD is only caused by your genetic inheritance
There is a strong inheritance of ADHD (60–70 per cent of children with diagnosed ADHD will have a family history of ADHD-type behaviours), but early environmental risk factors may explain up to 40 per cent of ADHD diagnoses.

Myth 3: ADHD is only present in boys
In childhood more boys than girls are diagnosed with ADHD, at a ratio of 4:1. This changes to 1.5:1 in adulthood, suggesting

that females are under diagnosed in childhood due to the type of ADHD they typically have (being quiet and inattentive rather than hyperactive), which is harder to diagnose.

Myth 4: ADHD can be easily diagnosed in very young children
ADHD can be difficult to diagnose in preschool children as they commonly have normal behaviour for their age. It is also necessary to rule out rarer conditions such as global developmental delay, autism, speech delay or hearing loss before making a diagnosis of ADHD.

Myth 5: ADHD only affects children
Longer-term studies have confirmed that childhood ADHD symptoms continue to some degree into adolescence and adulthood in around two thirds of individuals. Of all the children diagnosed and treated for ADHD, one third will not have symptoms in adulthood and will function normally, one third may not need medication in adulthood but will benefit from extra support, and one third will need medication and support into adulthood. The symptoms of ADHD can change in adolescence and adulthood; hyperactive children can become less hyperactive but, for some, inattention and distractibility can remain into their mid–30s.

Myth 6: ADHD can be diagnosed by anyone
The diagnosis of ADHD in children is complex, and must be made by a paediatrician, psychiatrist, or clinical/school psychologist with assistance from their teacher, general practitioner and allied therapist (speech therapist, occupational therapist, physiotherapist or life coach). Specific parent and teacher questionnaires need to be completed, including psychometric assessments by a clinical and/or school psychologist.

Myth 7: ADHD is due to poor parenting

It is known that poor parenting can cause bad behaviour, but with ADHD the child's difficult behaviour can make good parenting look-poor. Parents of children with ADHD often have their own mental health issues, which can further add to the challenges of parenting and family stress, hence they need to look after themselves. Since ADHD is to a certain degree heritable, one or both parents may have this condition, although it is often undiagnosed.

Myth 8: ADHD is mostly a solo diagnosis

ADHD is rarely a solo diagnosis as it usually presents with other conditions (learning difficulties, anxiety disorder, depression, oppositional defiant behaviour, conduct disorder, aggression, mood dysregulation disorder, developmental coordination disorder, motor or vocal tics and autism). These can change in severity through childhood, adolescence and adulthood, so it is important that these other conditions are recognised and managed appropriately.

Myth 9: Children with ADHD have similar brain structure and connections to their non-ADHD peers

Children with ADHD may have reduced brain volume and imma-ture connections as seen on an MRI scan. Their brain volume does increase to the normal adult size and the immature connections do normalise in their twenties, although their emotional development is typically 2–4 years behind what would be expected for their age.

Myth 10: Sleep difficulty in children with ADHD is only due to their stimulant medication

Difficulty falling asleep is common in children with ADHD, even before they start medication. Excluding other causes that may be contributing to sleep difficulty (e.g. anxiety, obstructive sleep apnoea, noise), and trying strategies such as keeping a routine, allowing no electronics in the bedroom or before sleep and regular exercise may be beneficial.

Myth 11: Stimulant medication makes children with ADHD short and skinny

Children diagnosed with ADHD and treated with stimulant medication may initially lose weight, but for most children this is a temporary phenomenon and the main problem in adult life is managing excess weight gain. Occasionally stimulant medication may affect growth. Studies have shown that children may have a final height 1 cm below what might have been their expected. It is important to have your child's height and weight closely monitored.

Myth 12: Medication is the only answer to treating your child with ADHD

Medication can help reduce the core symptoms of ADHD in 80 per cent of children and should be used in children who have moderate to severe symptoms. Having an age-appropriate healthy diet, including omega 3 fatty acids, and reducing food additives, if diagnosed with food intolerance, can help. Increasing exercise and contact with nature, assistance with behaviour, having a routine, supporting your child and managing some of the other conditions associated with ADHD can be beneficial before medication is started. However, the combination of a healthy, supportive lifestyle and medication can be very successful. However, there are a number of other ways of reducing ADHD symptoms which should be considered. Avoiding unhealthy dietary patterns (usually high in saturated fat, refined sugars, processed food and low in fruit and vegetables), reduce food additives and increase omega 3 fatty acids.

Myth 13: Medication has no long-term benefits

Stimulant medication has been shown to reduce the risk of serious head injuries and reduce the risk of children entering the juvenile justice system. Medication has also been shown to improve family functioning and classroom behaviour, although some studies have shown more medium-term than long-term benefits. More studies are urgently required in this area.

Myth 14: Medication will solve all of my child's learning problems

Approximately 30–40 per cent of children with ADHD also have a learning difficulty which can affect their literacy and numeracy skills. The medication will help them stay focused but does not necessarily directly help with their dyslexia. Dyslexia is usually managed with a specialised literacy program, and this can be done via the school through an individual education plan. However, the reality is that if your child has severe dyslexia, school programs may not be sufficiently intensive to adequately help them. We would encourage you to use both the school program and outside of school private literacy programs for more severe dyslexia, and private tutor or group tuition for less severe learning difficulties.

Myth 15: Every child with inattention and poor concentration has ADHD

This is certainly not the case as there are a number of other conditions which may mimic ADHD symptoms – for example, hearing and vision problems, sleep difficulty, epilepsy, poor nutrition, recreational drugs and alcohol.

Myth 16: Behaviour programs and/or special diet alone are effective for managing ADHD

This may be possible for children with mild ADHD symptoms but not for moderate to severe symptoms of ADHD. Medication is the most effective treatment for children with ADHD, but it is best used in conjunction with a range of other non-pharmacological treatments.

Myth 17: Corporal punishment is a successful approach to behaviour issues in children with ADHD

This is not the case – a number of studies have found that using physical force on children with or without ADHD can lead to long lasting mental health problems.

Myth 18: ADHD drugs are addictive

ADHD drugs are not addictive, especially when used in low doses. They are very different to methamphetamine (ice), which is addictive.

Myth 19: ADHD is diagnosed in children with bad behaviour

Most children diagnosed with ADHD are usually well behaved but find it hard to start and complete tasks, get distracted easily and often lack insight into how much they miss. The 'bad behaviour' is often related to your child with ADHD not being able to control their emotions when they become frustrated or stressed. Anxiety can also be displayed as very difficult and erratic behaviour, and sensory overload can also be displayed as aggression.

Myth 20: Children with ADHD have a low IQ

Although having ADHD may reduce some of your child's IQ sub-scores, especially their working memory and processing of information, they can have an IQ anywhere in the usual range, from low or average to high.

Twenty tips for parents

1. **Fit your own oxygen mask first.** Parenting is challenging. When a child has ADHD the task of parenting becomes even more so, and a specialised set of skills is required. It is vital for parents to take care of themselves as they take care of their children. Having a child with ADHD puts a strain on parents' relationships, so take care of your relationship as well.

2. **Children with ADHD need their parents to be organised.** Some parents are natural organisers; others find it challenging. If you are not an organised parent, get support from a friend or ADHD coach in order to improve your skills. Routines and systems will benefit your child and entire family, and will lighten the parenting load.

3. **Build a strong relationship with your child and develop trust.** It's natural for parents of a child with ADHD to focus on teaching as much as possible in order to provide them with the skills required to navigate life. Remember also to spend some time just being together. Your child will be learning valuable skills in this time. Trust them and earn their trust.

4. **Educate yourself about ADHD and coexisting conditions.** Knowledge is power – arm yourself well. ADHD is the most researched mental health condition in childhood. It is also the most sensationalised. Choose reliable sources with information based on research. Once you are educated, you can educate others.

142

5.   **Educate your child about ADHD and their own uniqueness.** Your child is so much more than an ADHD diagnosis. He or she is an individual with unique qualities. Be curious with your child, and discover their strengths, passions and dreams. Then, help your child to recognise how ADHD affects the way they operate. There is no 'one size fits all'.

6.   **Develop and maintain a DIY manual and a success diary.** Record information about your child in a document all about them. Include their special qualities, as well as successful strategies and motivators. This will become their DIY manual for managing their ADHD in the future. Keep a section for recording successes, big and small.

7.   **Be consistent, and expect inconsistency from your child.** Accept that your child will have good and bad days. Your child is not being lazy if they forget a skill they have previously mastered. Celebrate the good days and use them to motivate your child on the bad days. Understand that they find this frustrating and embarrassing too.

8.   **Manage transitions.** Children with ADHD have great difficulty switching their attention from one task to another, particularly when required to switch from a highly stimulating task to one that is less engaging. In addition to the many daily transitions, there are also major events that can cause problems for people with ADHD, such as moving to a different year of school, moving from primary to high school and from high school to university or TAFE,

or moving house. All transitions, big or small, require planning, warning and bridging activities.

9. **Teach your child to pause through mindfulness.** There is no pause button in an ADHD brain. Whatever captures your child's attention will become their priority. By teaching your child a simple mindfulness activity, you can demonstrate the power of a pause. With practice, this skill will become easier, and will give your child space to plan their next step.

10. **Manage emotional flooding.** Difficulty controlling emotions is a strong characteristic of ADHD, and this affects thoughts and actions. Your child will struggle with self-soothing, resulting in angry outbursts, brooding and/or mental meltdowns. Make your child aware that this is part of ADHD and have some agreed-upon strategies to help them work through it.

11. **Teach social skills and foster friendships.** Social interactions can be difficult for children with ADHD. Model social skills in your interactions. Find your 'tribe' of friendly families. Encourage friendship with children of all ages, rather the concentrating on their peer group. Set up short play dates with one friend at a time.

12. **Make time visible.** ADHD causes 'time blindness'. In order to make time manageable for your child, you will need to make it visible, and sometimes audible too. Use visual timers to keep track of time and create short sprints

to get tasks done. Weekly and monthly planners provide a picture of due dates and make it easier to assign time to tasks.

13. **Externalise your child's memory at the point of performance.** While children with ADHD often have excellent long-term memories, they struggle to hold information in their short-term working memory. Strategies, reminders, rewards and consequences must always be targeted at the point of performance. This includes reminders at the relevant time and place, as well as instant rewards for tasks completed successfully.

14. **Chunk and sprint.** Because of their inability to break tasks down, children with ADHD often become overwhelmed by what they perceive to be an enormous task. Instead of telling them to tidy their rooms, for example, break it down into a list of tasks, and use a timer to create 15/20/30-minute sprints. ADHD brains are great sprinters. If they can see a finish line, they are more likely to get started.

15. **Have systems to manage 'stuff'.** An untidy environment creates an untidy mind. ADHD brains need a tidy, organised environment in order to operate effectively. While children may claim that they know where everything is, be guided instead by the amount of time they spend looking for misplaced items. Find a balance between the level of tidiness they require, and the level of untidiness you can tolerate. Keep systems simple and design them with your child's input.

16. **Manage screens and technology.** The digital age brings many positives for children with ADHD. For example, computers make writing easier for many, apps are useful organising tools, and resources can be provided online by schools. However, these screens also create huge distractions, and sometimes addiction. Have clear guidelines about screen usage and lead by example. Seek professional help if you suspect your child has an addiction to screens.

17. **Inform the school and ask for support.** While some parents choose not to disclose their child's ADHD diagnosis, the ideal situation is for the school to be informed and have formal support in place. Provide evidence-based information about ADHD and any coexisting conditions that may affect your child. Also provide copies of assessments and reports. Ensure all teachers in the school are aware of your child's strengths and challenges.

18. **Develop realistic and healthy homework routines.** Clarify homework expectations with the school and ensure they are reasonable. Set aside a regular time each day for your child to complete assigned homework and assignments. Chunk tasks and create sprints. Help with prioritising and planning homework tasks. Have checks in place to keep your child off social media and other distracting internet sites during the homework period. Plan an instant reward at the end of homework. If homework becomes too stressful, employ a homework tutor.

19.   **Advocate for your child and teach self-advocacy.**
Ideally, you want your child to learn to ask for assistance
and accommodations. This skill will take some time for
your child to master. Be their advocate, modelling the skills
required until they have sufficient confidence, assertiveness
and awareness of what support they require to step up.
Teachers are always willing to help, but are often not aware
of the best way to support children who learn differently.
Help your child to identify effective accommodations, and
rehearse conversations they will have with their teachers
when making requests.

20.   **Build a village for your child.** We have all heard the
saying: 'It takes a village to raise a child'. When your child
has ADHD it may be harder to find that village, but it is
even more important. As your child makes the transition
into the adult world, they may not have acquired all the
skills they need. However, they may want their parents to
be less involved in their lives. It is important for your child
to have a group of trusted adults to call on.

Twenty tips for teachers

1. **Educate yourself about ADHD, coexisting conditions, and individual students.** Children with ADHD vary in the type of symptoms they display (dreamy or hyperactive, or both). The symptoms of ADHD, associated executive-function impairments and added learning disorders and/or mental health conditions such as anxiety, make it harder for them to learn. They experience great difficulties with organisation and time management. Parents are always a good source of information about their children. In addition, regular professional development in this area is important, as ADHD is the most commonly diagnosed condition in children.

2. **Be discreet.** There is significant stigma that accompanies a diagnosis of ADHD. Consequently, students and their families tend to limit disclosure of the diagnosis to those who need to know. Support your students by using discretion at all times. Have agreed-upon strategies and signals that are understood by you and the student in order to assist focus. Refrain from mentioning medication in the classroom or in front of others. Avoid shaming students for bad behaviour in front of other students.

3. **Expect inconsistency.** The behaviours and abilities of students with ADHD can vary from day to day, or throughout the day and across different learning contexts. This inconsistency, which can occur even when students are medicated, is sometimes interpreted as laziness or a lack

of effort. It is frustrating for teachers when students may be capable of a task one day, but not the next. It is even more frustrating for the students themselves. Celebrate and help them to record their successes as they provide useful data for facilitating future 'wins'. Avoid over-focusing on challenges.

4. **Showcase strengths.** While your students with ADHD may have gaps in their abilities, they will certainly have islands of competence, or even excellence. Provide opportunities for them to show their classmates that they are good at something.

5. **Ease transitions.** Students with ADHD require additional time and support to transition between environments and/or activities. In primary school, be flexible about transitions between activities. If a student who has taken longer to get started on an activity is focused when it is time to move on, consider allowing them more time to complete that activity. Also, help design a routine for settling back into classroom activities after recess and lunch break, and consider having that visible. In high school, be mindful that students will take longer to be focused at the start of a lesson.

6. **Brain dump.** When they find themselves focused, students are often reluctant to stop working, knowing how hard it will be to get started again. If at all possible, leave a focused student to complete a task. However, if work must stop, have students write down the next steps of the task. When they return, those notes will provide their next entry point.

7. **Allow fidgeting.** When students with ADHD are told to stop fidgeting, they spend a huge amount of mental energy concentrating on sitting still. Consequently, they find it hard to focus on what is being taught. In pre-primary and primary school, be tolerant of fidgeting that is not distracting others. In high school, teach your students discreet fidgets to overcome this problem. Doodling is a great fidgeting strategy, as is playing with a small piece of Blu Tack, or rubbing a small pebble. Have an agreement that students may leave the room for a bathroom break if they become restless.

8. **Chunk, and then dot point.** Teachers are great at chunking work for students. However, they often do not realise the level of chunking that needs to occur for students with ADHD. Because of their inability to break work down, students become overwhelmed by what they perceive to be an enormous task. In the classroom, giving students one task at a time or a short list of dot points creates an entry point, making it easier to get started. Assignments and projects should also be broken down into chunks.

9. **Sprint to get started.** ADHD brains are great sprinters. If they can see a finish line, they are more likely to get started. Help students create sprints by setting a 10/20/30-minute timer, and have them complete as much work as possible in that time. Along with sprints, frequent short breaks can be extremely effective. Allow your student to create a cycle of timed sprints and timed breaks to get through a large task.

10. **Take the load off working memory.** Make information visible in the classroom. Instructions and routines should be provided in writing. Allow students to photograph the board at the end of a lesson, and provide summaries of lessons if note taking is difficult. Make homework information and resources available for students and their parents on the school portal. Students with ADHD may be inconsistent with homework diaries and should be given support and accommodations in this area.

11. **Make time visible.** For students with ADHD there are two deadlines: work that is due *now* and work that is due *not-now*. They understand the timeframe of work that is due immediately, but not long-term projects. Have a planner on display with assignment due dates clearly marked. Cross off each day as it passes to give students a reference point. This creates a picture of the time available to them to complete a task. Encourage them to keep similar planners at home which include due dates of all assignments and out-of-school commitments.

12. **Encourage 'free-writing'.** Sometimes the best ideas get lost as students struggle to articulate them in an appropriate format or style. If this is the case, encourage students to get their ideas onto a page first and then arrange them into the appropriate format. This works best on a computer. For example, students might write the body of an essay first, and then go back to writing the introduction.

13. **Use white noise.** Allow students to listen to music, ambient sounds or white noise through earphones while working independently. This will block external and internal distractions. As a result, students will more easily focus on the task at hand. It will also prevent students from distracting others.

14. **Provide regular check-ins.** Encourage students to complete portions of assignments and discuss these with you before proceeding. Aside from the discussed benefits of chunking, this will keep them focused on the correct aspects, and prevent them from over-focusing on one aspect of the assignment to the detriment of others.

15. **Maintain regular communication with parents.** This can be done either via a communications book, particularly in primary school, or via email for students in high school. Remember to communicate the successes as well as the challenges experienced by students, as parents are often bombarded with complaints from the school. Do inform parents when assignments or long-term projects are assigned. Awareness of due dates enables parents to plan homework activities with their children.

16. **Foster friendships.** Students with ADHD find socialising difficult, due to their delayed emotional maturity. Encourage relationships with fellow students if possible. Be mindful when setting up group work to allow them to show their strengths. For example, if your student is a great 'brainstormer' but a poor writer, pair them with a talented scribe.

17. **Remain positive.** Children with ADHD have a lot of negative input in their lives from all directions, so try and use a 4:1 ratio, where four positive comments are made to one negative comment. Give more acknowledgement for appropriate behaviour than for inappropriate behaviour. Let's acknowledge that this can be challenging.

18. **Minimise distraction.** Minimise crowding with classroom materials, which can be quite distracting.

19. **Keep the student focused.** Sit the student in the front of the class close to the teacher's desk and repeat information in a way that is less distracting to the rest of class. (Attract the student's attention, maintain eye contact where possible, speak clearly using short sentences, use visual cues and wait for compliance if possible, pause between sentences and monitor student for 'blank looks'. Repeat instructions slowly and simply, and try not to expand too much.)

20. **Provide pre-class information.** If a new concept is being introduced into the class it would be best to inform the parents so that the topic can be discussed at home over the weekend, making new concepts easier to understand.

BIBLIOGRAPHY

American Psychiatric Association. *Diagnostic and statistical manual of mental disorders* (5th ed.). Arlington, VA: American Psychiatric Publishing, 2013.

Banerjee TD, Middleton F, Faraone SV. Environmental risk factors for attention-deficit hyperactivity disorder. *Acta Paediatr.* 2007;96:1269–74.

Barkley RA, Fischer M, Smallish L, Fletcher K. Young adult outcome of hyperactive children: adaptive functioning in major life activities. *J Am Acad Child Adolesc Psychiatry* 2006;45:192–202.

Bradley W. The behavior of children receiving benzedrine. *Am J Psychiat* 1937;94:577–85.

Brehaut JC, Miller A, Raina P, McGrail KM. Childhood behavior disorders and injuries among children and youth: a population-based study. *Pediatrics* 2003;111:262–9.

Canadian Attention Deficit Disorder Resource Allinance (CADDRA) (2011) *Canadian Practice Guidelines* (3rd ed.). Toronto Ontario: CADDRA, 2011.

Clinical practice guideline: diagnosis and evaluation of the child with attention-deficit/hyperactivity disorder. American Academy of Pediatrics. *Pediatrics* 2000;105:1158–70.

Coghill DR, Seth S, Pedroso S, Usala T, Currie J, Gagliano A. Effects of methylphenidate on cognitive functions in children and adolescents with attention-deficit/hyperactivity disorder: evidence from a systematic review and a meta-analysis. *Biol Psychiatry* 2013 DOI: 10.1016/j.biopsych.2013.10.005.

Danckaerts M, Sonuga-Barke EJ, Banaschewski T, Buitelaar J, Dopfner M, Hollis C, et al. The quality of life of children with attention deficit/

154

hyperactivity disorder: a systematic review. *Eur Child Adolesc Psychiatry* 2010;19:83–105.

Daughton JM, Kratochvil CJ. Review of ADHD pharmacotherapies: advantages, disadvantages, and clinical pearls. *J Am Acad Child Adolesc Psychiatry* 2009;48:240–8.

Efron D, Davies S, Sciberras E. Current Australian pediatric practice in the assessment and treatment of ADHD. *Acad Pediatr* 2013;13:328–33.

Efron D and Toner M. Transition to adult care for patients with ADHD. *ADHD in Practice* 2014;2(3).

Faraone SV. Using meta-analysis to compare the efficacy of medications for attention-deficit/hyperactivity disorder in youths. *P & T: a peer-reviewed journal for formulary management* 2009;34:678–94.

Felder RM and Spurlin J. Applications, reliability and validity of the Index of Learning Styles. *International Journal on Engineering Education* 2005;21(1):103–112.

Finlay F and Furnell C. Internet addiction disorder and ADHD. *ADHD in Practice* 2014;6(1).

Frederickson B. *Positivity*. London: Oneworld Publications, 2012.

Germanò E, Gagliano A, Curatolo P. Comorbidity of ADHD and Dyslexia. *Developmental Neuropsychology* 2010;35:475–93.

Giwerc, D. *Permission to proceed: creating a life of passion, purpose and possibility for adults with ADHD*. New York: ADD Coach Academy, 2011.

Goraya JS, Cruz M, Valencia I, Kaleyias J, Khurana DS, Hardison HH, et al. Sleep study abnormalities in children with attention deficit hyperactivity disorder. *Pediatr Neurol* 2009;40:42–6.

Hallowell E. *Crazy busy*. New York, Ballantine Books, 2006.

Harrison E. *The Foundations of mindfulness*. New York, The Experiment, 2017.

Johnston C, Mash EJ. Families of children with attention-deficit/hyperactivity disorder: review and recommendations for future research. *Clin Child Fam Psychol Rev* 2001;4:183–207.

Keenan HT, Hall GC, Marshall SW. Early head injury and attention deficit hyperactivity disorder: retrospective cohort study. *BMJ* 2008;337:a1984.

Kim HH, Viner-Brown SI, Garcia J. Children's mental health and family functioning in Rhode Island. *Pediatrics* 2007;119 Suppl 1:S22–8.

Kooij SJ, Bejerot S, Blackwell A, Caci H, Casas-Brugue M, Carpentier PJ, et al. European consensus statement on diagnosis and treatment of adult ADHD: The European Network Adult ADHD. *BMC Psychiatry* 2010;10:67.

Langley K, Rice F, van den Bree MB, Thapar A. Maternal smoking during pregnancy as an environmental risk factor for attention deficit hyperactivity disorder behaviour. A review. *Minerva Pediatr* 2005;57:359–71.

Millichap JG. Etiologic classification of attention-deficit/hyperactivity disorder. *Pediatrics* 2008;121:e358–65.

The MTA Cooperative Group. A 14-month randomized clinical trial of treatment strategies for attention-deficit/hyperactivity disorder. Multimodal treatment study of children with ADHD. *Arch Gen Psychiatry* 1999;56:1073–86.

NICE guideline, Attention deficit hyperactivity disorder: The NICE guideline on diagnosis and management of ADHD in children, young people and adults. *London: The British Psychological Society and The Royal College of Psychiatrists* 2008.

Nigg J, Nikolas M, Burt SA. Measured gene-by-environment interaction in relation to attention-deficit/hyperactivity disorder. *J Am Acad Child Adolesc Psychiatry* 2010;49:863–73.

O'Connor MJ, Shah B, Whaley S, Cronin P, Gunderson B, Graham J. Psychiatric illness in a clinical sample of children with prenatal alcohol exposure. *Am J Drug Alcohol Abuse* 2002;28:743–54.

Pearce C. *A short introduction to promoting resilience in children*. London: Jessica Kingsley Publisher, 2011.

Plomp E, Van Engeland H, Durston S. Understanding genes, environment and their interaction in attention-deficit hyperactivity disorder: is there a role for neuroimaging? *Neuroscience* 2009;164:230–40.

Polanczyk G, de Lima MS, Horta BL, Biederman J, Rohde LA. The worldwide prevalence of ADHD: a systematic review and metaregression analysis. *Am J Psychiatry* 2007;164:942–8.

Prescott S and Logan A. *The Secret life of Your Microbiome*. New Society Publishers. 2017.

Ríos-Hernández A, Alda J, Farran-Codina A, Ferreira-García E, Izquierdo-Pulido M. The Mediterranean Diet and ADHD in Children and Adolescents. *Pediatrics* 139 : 2:2017.

Seligman M. *Authentic happiness.* London: Hodder & Stoughton, 2011.

Shaw P, Malek M, Watson B, Sharp W, Evans A, Greenstein D. Development of cortical surface area and gyrification in attention-deficit/hyperactivity disorder. *Biol Psychiat* 2012;72(3).

Silva D, Colvin L, Hagemann E, Bower C. Environmental risk factors by gender associated with attention-deficit/hyperactivity disorder. *Pediatrics* 2013.

Silva D, Colvin L, Hagemann E, Stanley F, Bower C. Children diagnosed with attention deficit disorder and their hospitalisations: population data linkage study. *Eur Child Adolesc Psychiatry* 2014 DOI 10.1007/s00787-014-0545-8.

Silva DT, Houghton S, Bower C. Child attention deficit hyperactive disorder co-morbidities on family stress: effect of medication. *Community Mental Health Journal* 2014.

Sonuga-Barke EJ, Brandeis D, Cortese S, Daley D, Ferrin M, Holtmann M, et al. Nonpharmacological interventions for ADHD: systematic review and meta-analyses of randomized controlled trials of dietary and psychological treatments. *Am J Psychiatry* 2013;170:275–89.

Thapar A, Cooper M, Jefferies R, Stergiakouli E. What causes attention deficit hyperactivity disorder? *Arch Dis Child* 2012;97:260–5.

Toner M, O'Donoghue T, Houghton S. Living in chaos and striving for control: how adults with attention deficit hyperactivity disorder deal with their disorder. *International Journal of Disability, Development and Education* 2006;53(2):247–261.

Willcutt EG, Pennington BF, Olson RK, Chhabildas N, Hulslander J. Neuropsychological analyses of comorbidity between reading disability and attention deficit hyperactivity disorder: in search of the common deficit. *Developmental neuropsychology* 2005;27:35–78.

Yoshimasu K, Barbaresi WJ, Colligan RC, Voigt RG, Killian JM, Weaver AL, et al. Childhood ADHD is strongly associated with a broad range of psychiatric disorders during adolescence: a population-based birth cohort study. *J Child Psychol Psychiatry* 2012;53:1036–43.

Young S, Amarasinghe JM. Practitioner review: Non-pharmacological treatments for ADHD: a lifespan approach. *J Child Psychol Psychiatry* 2010;51:116–33.

ACKNOWLEDGEMENTS

The authors would like to thank Brad Jongeling, Emma Scriberras, Jan Herrington, Jenny Brockis, Wai Chen and Elizabeth Spencer Fawell for their valuable feedback during the manuscript preparation. Also, their thanks go to Andrea Scott for her assistance with the manuscript layout. Most importantly, they would like to acknowledge all the children, parents and teachers who inspired them to write this book. Last, but by no means least, they are thankful for the support and encouragement they received from their families over the many months of writing, editing, and publishing their *ADHD Go-To Guide*.

CPSIA information can be obtained
at www.ICGtesting.com
Printed in the USA
BVOW03s0015181117
500040BV00008B/2/P